A TIME
OF
HUMANITIES

West Bend Art Museum
300 South 6th Avenue
West Bend, WI 53095
Non-Profit Organization

David H. Stevens

A TIME OF HUMANITIES

An Oral History
Recollections of David H. Stevens
as Director in the
Division of the Humanities,
Rockefeller Foundation, 1930-50

as narrated to Robert E. Gard
by David H. Stevens

edited by Robert E. Yahnke

and an essay
What Are the Humanities?
by David H. Stevens

West Bend
Art Museum
Collection

First Edition
ISBN 0-88361-042-6

Library of Congress Card Number 76-22968

Copyright 1976 by the Wisconsin Academy of Sciences, Arts and Letters.

Published by the Wisconsin Academy of Sciences, Arts and Letters in association
with Wisconsin House Book Publishers.
Printed in the United States of America by Straus Printing & Publishing Co., Inc.,
Madison, Wisconsin.

Contents

Introduction

The Division for the Humanities of the Rockefeller Foundation was established officially in 1928, when the Foundation reorganized its structure and transferred programs in the humanities from the General Education Board to the Rockefeller Foundation itself. The General Education Board had been set up in 1902 for the "promotion of education within the United States of America, without distinction of race, sex, or creed." Throughout the next thirty years, the GEB concentrated its efforts on improving elementary, secondary, and higher education for all people in the United States, especially in the South. Some of the specific aids to education supported by the Board were an increase of teachers' salaries, the construction of new school buildings, libraries, and laboratories, and the support of educational research. Although the GEB did not make substantial moves into the humanities, it did initiate in 1924 a series of grants in the humanities in the areas of archeology, the fine arts, and research. In 1927 it made large five-year grants available to several prominent universities in order to stimulate general programs in the humanities.

This was the General Education Board that David Stevens joined in 1930 after twenty-two years of teaching and administrative work at Northwestern University and the University of Chicago. Stevens became vice-president of the GEB at the age of forty-six. Much of his early work was centered on helping to maintain the Southern program of the GEB, the plan to aid black education in the South by supporting equally black and white education. When Stevens moved over to the Rockefeller Foundation in 1932 and became director for Humanities, he had an opportunity to change the direction of Foundation support for the humanities by emphasizing the development of new ideas and new programs.

Robert Gard was a graduate student at Cornell University, working under Alexander Drummond, when he first met David Stevens. Out of that meeting Gard received Rockefeller Foundation fellowships from 1938-1940, and this began an association with David Stevens and the Foundation that extended through the next thirty-five years and included work in community drama, folklore, and arts research. Gard has been at the University of Wisconsin since 1945 and is a well-known author and originator of the Wisconsin Idea Theatre and the Wisconsin Regional Writers Association.

His idea to compile an oral history of Stevens' years as director of the Division for the Humanities grew out of his long friendship with David

Stevens. In 1974 Gard began the project by talking with Stevens at length over several days and recording their conversations. These interviews led to a substantial manuscript, which was added to after another series of interviews. In the summer of 1975 the Rockefeller Foundation agreed to provide support for a proposed oral history, and the University of Wisconsin-Extension Arts received a six-month grant to develop the materials into final book form. Because I had helped to prepare the initial manuscripts by transcribing the tapes and editing the transcripts into a readable form, I came into the project as editor for the term of the grant.

A Time of Humanities, the oral history based on these interviews, begins with "Background to the Humanities." Here Stevens explores the sources of his growth as a humanist by recalling the importance of close family ties and the emphasis given to education in his early years. He continues with recollections of his study in college, his experiences at the University of Chicago as teacher and administrator, and his work in the General Education Board and the Rockefeller Foundation.

In the second part of the oral history, "Men and Ideas," Stevens reviews the progress made toward opening new areas of research and self-expression for the humanist in the 1930's and 1940's. He begins with examples of how the raw materials of research were made available to the scholar. After explaining the principles and methods of Foundation operation, he presents three chapters describing programs of particular concern to him when he became director of the Division: Far Eastern studies, American studies, and drama. In these chapters he also comments on the impact of the depression and World War II on individuals and Foundation programs. To conclude the oral history, Stevens surveys programs completed after World War II, defines the role of the foundation in contemporary life, and emphasizes the development of a sense of values as the basis for educating a humanist.

The focus in "Men and Ideas" is on the importance of developing brilliant young humanists who, if given sufficient support, can initiate new programs. There are numerous examples, throughout his narrative, of young men and women who were given a chance and who succeeded. In order to add to the historical significance of the oral history, Gard and I decided to contact as many of these people as possible and to ask them for any informal reminiscences they might have concerning their involvement with the Foundation or with David Stevens. We received more than twenty responses. These brief commentaries are placed within the narrative, in most cases immediately following Stevens' discussion of their programs, so that another dimension may be added to *A Time of Humanities.* (Biographical information on these individuals is presented in brief sketches of the contributors, at the end of the text.)

Accompanying the oral history is David Stevens' formal statement of the substance and continuing purpose of the humanities. "What Are the Humanities?" complements *A Time of Humanities* by acknowledging the initiative and dedication of individual teachers, scholars, and researchers, who have carried on the tradition of human learning and experience so that future generations may enjoy a more meaningful existence. At the same time, Stevens' essay shows the power of the humanities to develop character, increase knowledge, and invigorate the spirit. In their final form, both *A Time of Humanities* and "What Are the Humanities?" stand as expressions not only of David Stevens' deep concern for the individual as humanist, but as significant comments on the development of the humanities to this day.

Robert E. Yahnke

Part One
Background to the Humanities

The White Sands of La Jolla retirement hotel is low and long, on the street side. Vines cling on walls above small balconies, and red bougainvillaea is in bloom in late October. At the back the building meanders down the slope almost to the beach, where the Pacific surf runs in high, broken a half-mile out by a reef. Lobster boats come to the reef each day, and on the terrace above the sea there are walks, gardens, and benches where the residents of the White Sands often come to rest and talk.

Earlier this morning I have walked on the terrace with my friend Stevens. He is ninety-one, I younger by many years, but not younger either. We have watched children on the beach, a small dog chasing and fetching, a young couple holding hands. During our walk he has commented on many things, including adventures we have had together. Once we spent months in Finland on a job, and we exchange accounts and news of many people we both know there. We talk about our homes in Wisconsin, where we both reside officially, he at Ephraim, I at Madison. We speak of his wife, Ruth, who died the year before, and we return to his room, for we must begin another assignment we have undertaken together.

His room is small, quiet, comfortable: a few cherished pictures, a painting of wild geese landing on a marsh. There is a large desk, an electric portable typewriter resting on the pull-out shelf. A long side-table, with fruit his daughter had brought the evening before, also has many books on it. There are two chairs, a small end-table between them, and the *New York Times Book Review* is spread open on the desk. Everything is convenient, comfortable, easy.

We will converse today of men in search, of human needs, of humanities programs in governments and institutions, of the shaping of human talent. He speaks clearly, with force still. As he speaks, his penetrating, yet warm eyes brighten with remembered challenge, with kindled recollection of place and persons. We set the recorder on the end table between us. I think he is perhaps a little apprehensive, for our conversations of the past have never had such firm purpose of systematic recall. . . .

1. SOURCES OF THE HUMANITIES

I. Early Years

GARD: David, I know that you have always been interested in men and ideas. I remember the time back in 1945 at the Prince George Hotel, when I was attending a National Theatre Conference meeting in New York, you said to me, "Well, why don't you talk to these delegates about *ideas*?"

I didn't do it then, but I thought about it and I knew what you were talking about. You wanted me to bring ideas into focus that had strength and meaning for the arts . . . ideas that required courage, vividness, imagination to put into gear.

STEVENS: Of course, the humanities would never exist except in people. They have value only as they may be interpreted through another person. When you look backward and estimate the record of humanity, it has to be reinterpreted in every generation. So the people who think that social studies or science are the impress of humanity don't realize how the whole turmoil of human record is represented and must be re-presented in terms of each generation. Each individual who interprets the past or present, or just interprets his imaginary grasp of those things, not only preserves and re-presents, but recreates himself.

GARD: David, how long did it take you to develop that viewpoint about the humanities? I know that you have always been in scholarly work, but when and how did a wide view of the humanities materialize for you?

STEVENS: I suppose through experience. I worked with people as a young instructor at the University of Chicago, and later I was a dean and met plenty of students. After all, I taught at Chicago from 1912 to 1930. The last four years I worked with Max Mason as assistant to the president, and I stayed on there after Bob Hutchins came. I met not only the young people, but the trustees and all types of persons in the University and in the community.

The tradition of the University of Chicago is part of it, too, because when I went there in 1912 as a graduate student and taught my way through two years for my degree, Chicago still was Harper's university. You could walk on the campus and an older man would stop you and say, "What's *your* name?" When you told him, he would say, "I'm *Mister* so-and-so." He never said "professor" or "doctor." It was a human institution—no frills. And then he would ask what your work was, and likely say, "Well, you may not be acquainted with him, but there's a man I know who has some excellent material in your field. It might be of some help to you." Then he told you who it was. The faculty took a personal interest in you. I would say that if you are interested in ideas, and in the people who generate them, and if you can help to get people started on important work, well, that's what your job is.

GARD: I think, from what you've told me during visits in the past, that your early boyhood, the kind of home you were in, your relationship with your brother and sister, were the things that had a profound influence in shaping you, too.

STEVENS: Of course. I grew up in a Civil War family. My father lost his father in the Civil War, and my mother lost her brother. Both of them were pretty much on their own after the war. Mother was a country girl living outside Mount Union in central Pennsylvania. They were poor enough so that when she went to town — usually to church or Sunday school — she always carried her shoes. She carried them to the edge of town; then she would put them on.

My father's father was killed in the Battle of the Wilderness. My father got the news while he was out fishing. He threw his fish pole in the brook, went home, and set to work running the farm. He was fourteen at the time. He had three sisters and a brother, and they all worked a stony hill in the center of Pennsylvania. Uncle Frank had been in the Battle of the Wilderness, too, and when my grandfather, David, was killed, Frank buried him on the field in his own blanket.

My father clerked in his store and met my mother in the Methodist church of that town. Uncle Frank sent my father through Dickinson University and then on through Drew Theological Seminary in New Jersey. The day mother and he were married they got aboard a train to come to Wisconsin, where father would start preaching. They had fifty dollars and two roasted chickens. That was about the extent of their wealth. They were on the way to Wausau, where he was to fill in after the tenure of a prominent minister. Wausau then was one of the best Methodist pastorates in the state.

Two of the towns that we lived in, and which I remember especially well, were Evansville and Fort Atkinson. The parsonage in Evansville was primitive in many respects — no central heating, but a coal-burning heater with isinglass in the doors around the coals and a warming oven in the back that was useful for warming doughnuts and keeping warm the "set" for morning pancakes. There was an outdoor toilet, and at the side of the house, a well with its two buckets for bringing up water.

I remember that when we moved on to Fort Atkinson, somewhat more advanced in style, our first visitors from Evansville were greeted at the front door with my invitation to come down into the cellar to see the furnace. But there we still had an outdoor toilet and an outdoor pump. In both towns we had a live-in servant for three dollars a week, and in winter there were always two barrels of apples, Jonathan and greenings, and a tub of corned beef that father made following his Pennsylvania training. Also, in both towns we three children trailed him around every Saturday night as he paid the week's bills, in order to gather small gifts of food or candy.

GARD: Your mother and father must have been remarkable people.

STEVENS: Mother was the daughter of an Irish weaver, strong in following her beliefs and dedicated to church work. From her father, and perhaps from some of their experiences of early years in Wisconsin towns, she became a determined worker for the W.C.T.U. and always wore a small bow of white ribbon as evidence of hostility to drink.

Perhaps the best instance of their experiences in this matter was the threat sent father by the saloon keepers of Berlin, Wisconsin, the town where I was born, that if he didn't stop preaching temperance they would put him on his back in the street and pour whiskey down his throat. But to resume about mother. I still can feel, mentally, the pressure of her temple against my own, and I remember nothing of my boyhood except her kindness and consideration for us all.

I remember father as always singing while walking about in the house, such religious songs, now out of date and out of all hymnals, doubtless, as "We're Marching to Zion!" and Bunyan's well-known pilgrim story beginning

> He who would valiant be
> 'Gainst all disaster,
> Let him in constancy
> Follow the Master!

He was a constant pastor of his people and a steady worker on his handwritten sermons before the days of typewriters.

It was in the small public library in Fort Atkinson that my brother and I read through all the books that we decided deserved our attention and constantly worked at music. I was about eleven years old when we moved to Fort Atkinson. There were two sisters in town named Snell; all the children in Fort Atkinson took music lessons from them. My brother studied piano and I the violin. We used to play for church services and for rural shows. I had a good grounding in music. The interesting thing today about this story is that my father, on a $1,800 salary, found a hundred dollars to buy me a violin made by a professional violin maker in Northampton, Massachusetts, by the name of Hyde.

GARD: These community home roots are profound in the way they affect us. I remember that my grandfather, who was a homestead farmer down in Kansas, planted the first flower garden in that part of Kansas, just because he wanted to see something beautiful growing in the yard. He too played the violin. I suppose he was just a kind of country fiddler, but they had music and they had flowers. I think that out of the crucible of the small town and the rural areas have come some of the deep things in our way of life.

STEVENS: Of course. It is part of the pioneer instinct that keeps people developing themselves. Well, after father bought the violin, he scraped up money to buy a piano for my sister and brother. Its arrival started a new kind of life for the entire family, with singing every morning after prayers.

6

Father ended up by becoming a district superintendent and living in Janesville, where my sister and I had the good fortune to have our last two years of high school in an excellent school. It was like an eastern preparatory school. Half of the teachers were from New England. There I had my third and fourth years of Latin, two of German, and one in Greek, as well as excellent courses in science.

GARD: David, looking back at your young life, specifically this early period we are talking about, how do you think your habits in reading and all that you had been exposed to in small towns affected your work when you became a humanist in Chicago?

STEVENS: In addition to the things I have mentioned, the greatest influence on my life as a boy was my brother Warren, four years older. He had a great sense of humor and was an artist, always drawing pen-and-ink sketches, caricatures, of people. We still have one drawn after hearing William Jennings Bryan campaign from the rear of a train in Fort Atkinson. The life in small towns, with plenty of time for reading standard classics and hearing older people who had time to talk with young ones, had special influences.

Another influence was living in a parsonage. We three children would watch, from a discreet distance, the weddings in the family parlor and, after each, hurry to ask father if the returns were three dollars or even more—as much as ten. We learned self-sacrifice from the examples of parents and a lot of understanding of the problems and hardships of others. It was a great education to be brought up with a brother and sister, of course.

GARD: Of course it is, and with a mother and father such as you had, and with a friendly nature, which I'm sure you had, it must have brought you into contact with all kinds of people in these communities.

David, one thing that was widely known about you when you were working with so many people for the Rockefeller Foundation was the fact that you appeared to have a deep understanding of people—particularly young people. You seemed to understand what they were striving for. I guess what interests me is how you were able to develop that sympathy out of that early crucible of experience we have been talking about.

STEVENS: I think some of it came from living in hard times with people who saved every nickel, hearing from father and mother stories that were before my time in their own lives, and seeing them follow their old Pennsylvania traditions. For example, their story of annual migrations to Camp Byron, near Fond du Lac, to meet friends from neighboring churches for camp meetings. Everyone brought his needed things for two weeks in camp, down to an iron cook stove on the rear of the wagon.

Father used to take us back to Pennsylvania in the summer, and after we had packed up a large trunk, we would live with relatives for a couple of months up in the mountains. The husbands of my father's three sisters were all in coal mining. We would go through a town named Orbisonia, where two of them lived, and walk all through the hills and mountains and learn a lot that way. But I still remember the hardships those miners suffered. They had to get up early, and I've been up more than once to eat breakfast with them. They had to eat a meal that would last them throughout the day. They would have pancakes, meat, and end up with pie. Then they would take a big tin can full of coffee along with their lunch. They were used to hardships.

I remember going back there years later with my wife, just to see the town, and we found one of the cousins still living in the old house. The town was so poor, even then, that when I tried to cash a traveler's check at the American Express office, the man said, "I haven't got that much money"—twenty dollars!

GARD: One more thing I want to talk about is the kind of local entertainment that you were exposed to in your boyhood, and some of the plays and church entertainments.

STEVENS: It was in Fort Atkinson that I had my earliest experiences in community arts. The local church was always a center of fellowship.

GARD: That's exactly right. I think that small churches contributed something to appreciation of the arts. They were often about the only places where people could hear choral music, or get some semblance of the visual arts in church decoration. And in addition the American Chautauqua movement was influential. There must have been Chautauquas playing in your towns in the summer.

STEVENS: Summers our parents would take us to the Chautauqua on Lake Monona in Madison. We would take our tent, set it up with an outdoor board bench to hold a two-burner gasoline stove, and hear such lectures as were in *Modern Eloquence*. At one of the special evenings I heard Remenyi, the famous violinist. There were classes in the mornings for us three children, and I am sure we heard Friday night lectures by fifteen or more leading speakers in the entire country.

About the biggest story I know about a Chautauqua was from the University of Chicago, when William Rainey Harper was its president. He didn't give up his connection with the Chautauqua in New York State. He went every Friday night and lectured. He taught there over the weekend and came back to his work at the University. George Vincent, who was a dean of the University at the same time, was Harper's first assistant. He told us about the unusual things that he and Harper engineered. This Chautauqua was one which grew very rapidly. It was so successful that the Methodist church started to buy land across the hill to put in another Chautauqua there. What Harper and Vincent did was to engage all the prominent speakers of that denomination for that next summer to speak at their Chautauqua. That killed the whole movement.

GARD: I remember the Chautauquas that came down and played in the Kansas towns. There were a great many little towns that had Chautauqua tents in them. I remember the town my grandmother and grandfather lived in, which couldn't have had more than three hundred people, and yet they had a Chautauqua.

I guess community entertainments are chiefly interesting because out of your attitude toward those things you get a kind of foreshadowing of what you might appreciate later on in life. That's why I've been asking you about these events. I remember the first play I saw — which nearly scared me to death — at Iola, Kansas. My brother was in it, and at one point he took a big pistol out of his pocket, and was going to shoot somebody with it. I thought sure this was real life. I couldn't separate it from fantasy at that time. My brother was just an actor, but he seemed like a real person.

When you got to be eighteen, or whenever it was that you graduated from high school, was it about that time that you three children moved to Appleton?

STEVENS: I followed my brother, Warren, who went to Lawrence College. He was a senior in my freshman year, and for the last year my brother was there, our father bought a house in Appleton. It had four rooms — two bedrooms, living room and kitchen. He paid seven hundred and fifty dollars for it. It still is in use, on Rankin Street. The next year he sold it, as a minister would, for the same sum—seven hundred and fifty dollars. This was, for that one year, a gathering place for all our friends.

GARD: You said earlier that your brother Warren was an important influence in your life. Could you elaborate on that?

STEVENS: It is difficult to imagine two brothers or two friends who are more completely intimate. Warren had a remarkable sense of humor and the finest eye for picking out oddities in people, which made him the kind of artist he was. He was a great observer and didn't talk too much, but he did things with his pencil and with his oral comment on circumstance and on people that made him a very unusual individual. He always had friends as a boy, and in college he had some friends that were completely devoted to him.

I suppose the simplest way to sum it up was that he sacrificed for the sake of the family and he sacrificed for me. He helped take care of my mother in a longstanding illness, stayed home, and never married. When I was running through graduate school on a shoestring and feeling I had to get to England to get the material to finish my thesis, he gave me the money. When I got back to Boston, without enough money left to tip any of the stewards or waiters, a check was there to get me back to Chicago.

II. University of Chicago

GARD: I'm sure that some of your ability to sympathize with the needs and goals of young people came from your early work in college teaching.

STEVENS: Well, I had my first chance when Northwestern University called me to teach Freshman English—with only a bachelor's degree and one year in a public school. As I walked on campus the first time, I was stopped by a pair of upperclassmen, to start me toward their fraternity. Then, as a cub teacher, I was given the drudgery class of "Pity sakes!"— student name for the clean-up course for the freshmen found too deficient to enter a regular unit of thirty in a section. On my first day a burly football candidate took a look from the door, muttered that he "wouldn't be taught by any kid," and left. But in a while he was back to work out his freedom.

That first-year course had Clark's *Practical Rhetoric,* made up of erroneous sentences, for reasons of grammar or simple word meaning. Our chairman had culled these out of papers of earlier students, and the result was sufficient to make a solid pack of bad specimens. There were thirty in a lesson, and these were to be served up during a full semester each day to two sections of thirty students. These were the primary indignities of Clark.

I had three years of this before I went off for a year of graduate study at Harvard University, and after doing my ten months down East, I came away with a Master's degree in English. It was a mixed lot of courses — Old English, Old French, a full year on English drama, a half year of a Chaucer seminar. I worked so hard that apart from rare weekend times away I studied.

Change to the University of Chicago was a release from this, and teaching provided an income for living while in graduate studies. We had 900 freshmen, and the kind of teaching I started with was one section of thirty students in a class, five days a week. Later I had two sections. These I carried along with my graduate work.

Every week for the first month Teddy Linn, a junior college dean, had a class session with his freshman teachers and told us *how* to teach. Some of these thirty never had taught. One of his very interesting admonitions was, "Your first class you're going to be scared. You may get rattled. So, in this first class take enough ammunition in notes to fill two hours, because if you get to talking too fast you'll run out; and the worst thing you can possibly do is to let a class of students out before the time is up." That's the way we started off.

GARD: You once told me that you knew John Manly while you were at Chicago.

STEVENS: Mr. Manly really brought me up, I suppose, and took me as a cub teacher when he found I was considering my first call to go out to teach as I took my doctor's degree. He said, "You don't have to do all the things you're asked to do," and at once I knew that was a forewarning of what I had hoped and anticipated, that I might became a member of his department. He didn't dictate; he was a man who led by example rather than by injunction. He worked constantly and he inspired people. Jim Hulbert wrote in his article in the *Dictionary of American Biography* that Manly "had the quality of stimulating people to achievement beyond their ordinary abilities." He had a particularly devoted staff, because he let them alone. When I got to talk to him about my thesis project, which I thought up and brought to him, he said, "Any time you want to talk anything over, just walk in."

Of course, what I have told you about so far are my earliest days at Chicago, when I was there as a cub instructor and a graduate student, and the spirit of Harper was still all through the University. They were still on a financing level whereby a professor had to do other things for the University in order to live. The head of the Greek department, Edward Capps, was also the head of the University Press. Harper had long-range vision that led always to deficits in budgets. When he asked a new man to head a department, he would say, "You come and I'll give you two journals—a popular one and a scholarly one." That's where the journal practice in American universities got its start. Hopkins did the same thing on a smaller scale. Well, one day Capps got word by telephone to be at the president's house the next morning at half past seven. When he got there he found also the head of the Latin department, Mr. Hale.

A University trustee was also there, and he said, "I had to see you before I went upstairs to talk to Harper. He's in bed. I want to tell you what I've got to tell him. We've decided that we've got to drop your journals—to save money." The trustee went in and when he came back he said, "I had to wait outside a while to get in. Before I got through the door, Harper called out, 'I know what you're here for. This fellow by the bed is my lawyer, and he's going to have dictation of a new will to endow those two journals.'" So the trustee told Capps and Hale, "You get out on the street, now, and raise three thousand dollars by Friday and we'll try to keep the journals." That happened, and they kept them.

GARD: What was the specific reason for raising the three thousand dollars?

STEVENS: Well, they had to pay the printing bill. There wouldn't be any issue that month if they didn't get the money.

GARD: So Harper's endowment would take care of the journals after he died?

STEVENS: That was a bluff, of course. He had his lawyer right beside his bed.

GARD: Harper wasn't dying?

STEVENS: Oh, no. No, he was putting the trustee on. He was bluffing him. He said, "You're going to kill those journals? I'll endow them!" That's the way he did business. That was just to stop the trustee from cutting off the journals. Then they had to go out and raise the money on it. The way the University Press ran was that it presumably had income, but then the amount of income was irregular, and their publication was determined by the income from the sale of their books. In those days, they didn't have much sale. The best book that Capps got out was the book by Jacques Loeb, the great biologist.

Capps told me a very good story concerning this, of when Mr. Rockefeller was giving, say, six hundred thousand or more—I don't know how much a year—to balance the budget. At that time he was trying to cut down the deficit; so he sent out a financial man to scout the University and to look over the next year's budget. When the Rockefeller agent came to the Press, he said, "Let me see your list of titles." These titles were in the list of manuscripts awaiting publication. He said, "Now here's this man, Loeb. Great biologist . . . scratch that one out—you don't have to take that one." Capps said, "Oh, no. That's all taken care of."

Well, before this incident, Capps had been to see Harper. Harper then was in the hospital. He called Capps over to his bed and said, "Now Loeb is leaving us. He has thirty assistants promised him. You have the manuscript that he wrote while he was here. We can't keep him, but he did that manuscript for Chicago; you have to publish it!" That closed the argument. And Capps, having no money, offhand said, "Oh, we'll take care of that. That's all taken care of." And so when this Rockefeller man came and wanted that manuscript scratched, Capps told me, "I knew I was on the spot—so I went to the bank, gave my own note for the money to publish that book for Jacques Loeb, and it came out under Chicago imprint on my money. It was such a great book that in three months we had all the money back."

Well, when I was in the University as a cub teacher, I knew men like Vincent, who became president of the University of Minnesota, then of the Rockefeller Foundation, and Trevor Arnett, a comptroller, who had made friends with Rockefeller people, chiefly John D., Jr. Trevor went to New York as the successor to Dr. Buttrick and became president of the General Education Board just a little before the reorganization of the Boards and the closing out of separate units, such as the work being done under Edmund Day in social sciences. Buttrick had been a minister in Minneapolis.

As a good Baptist, Frederick Gates knew John D., Jr. Finally, he was taken to New York to help John D. with his charities. It was then that the sparring began between Harper and Gates over how much a year John D., Sr. was going to give to the University or whether he would ever give anything. Harper held out, and he wouldn't go until he had a pretty firm promise of protection and subsidy.

In my day, Professor Max Mason had been brought from the University of Wisconsin. He was a brilliant research man. I had left my teaching and been his assistant for four years.

GARD: Could we pause a minute and circle back here a little bit, and then we'll go back and pick up at this point again. You knew Max Mason quite well, and he certainly was a colorful figure at the University of Wisconsin. Could you give any kind of characterization of him, in terms of the way he operated, how he looked, the way he spoke?

STEVENS: Tall, angular, very quick-motioned, not particularly fitted, perhaps, to be an executive of a university; but he had a great, great hold on Chicago. He and Harold Swift and I were very close friends and did many things together. Max was temperamentally unhappy, of course. He had left Wisconsin with some trouble behind him, and his wife was not stable; so Max had a hard time, in some ways, personally.

I remember particularly once when he came home from a business trip to New York. He said, "When I got off the New York Central in Englewood, to drive to the University, my nervous tension began, and I got these welts on my arm." This showed that he was nervous and unhappy, unstable. But he was a very exciting man. Every minute of conversation with Max was fun.

I recall we had been working together a while, and he had made a number of public speeches — one of them to a big audience in Mandel Hall — and the next day he got a letter from a woman who had heard the talk. She said, "I am a voice teacher. If you will come to my office in the Loop three or four times, I can tell you how to talk." She said, "You don't know how to control your voice." He was best in talking in a group. He did it beautifully. But he talked with his throat, not with his diaphragm, and did not project his voice. Well, he was curious, of course; but he ignored her advice.

He had been making his talks for a while, and I said, "Max, we have to get you a new speech. You start half of them with that same old story about the dog. Your dog needed medicine, so you got the boys lined up and got a big tablespoon and castor oil, and they held him. You put it down the dog's throat; he shook himself, and came over and licked the

13

spoon." He said, "That's my idea of education. Give it to them, and they'll find out that they do like it." Max's argument was not simply let the student go easy, as progressive education and some of the people in California are saying nowadays — "let him go way up to ten or twelve years without trying to discipline his mind" — which is the extreme of John Dewey's idea. Max Mason's idea was, find out what is good for him and he'll take it.

Well, I said to Max, "You've got to get a new speech." So every day now and then for ten days I would stop at the door and say, "Well, when are we going to start that speech?" One day I opened the door, and there he was, pacing up and down the big room, a girl taking down notes, and he said, "Get out of here, Dave, I'm writing that speech!"

Another incident in his office was on one day when he got to talking about religion, and his idea of eternity. Looking out the window, with his eyes staring off into the future, he suddenly turned on me and said, "You don't think I'm religious, do you?" And I said, "Sure I do, if you say so." He was really an odd personality—part genius.

GARD: You got along with him quite well, didn't you?"

STEVENS: Oh, yes. One day a trustee came in and said, "Max, you must come over to the Baptist church this morning. You've got to join the Baptist church." He said, "What the hell do you mean?" "Well," the trustee said, "the proportion of Baptists on the Board must remain constant. In order to invite the new trustee we want, we have to make you a Baptist." So they did.

Another example of his whimsical personality. Merriam, the great professor of economics and politics, came in one day, sat down and said, "Max, I see on your desk piles of paper on your left and piles of paper on the right. What's the difference?" "Oh," Max said, "these are the important and those are the more important. I shift them back and forth now and then."

Another very colorful incident was when the University was angling for money for the Medical School. Abe Flexner, who was then still active with Arnett in the office of the General Education Board, as its secretary, also did a venture here and there for the medical purposes of the Rockefeller Foundation. He sent word ahead: "Max, I want your time exclusively—not to be interrupted for a whole day—to talk over these problems you have on the future of the Medical School." He was a rather arrogant and possessive gentleman. I know many instances to establish the adjectives—such as his rude greeting to another officer before others: "Hello! Are you half as smart as you think you are?"

Well, during that day I telephoned a question to Max. Flexner may not have liked it, but I really didn't care about anything except settling an important university problem. When he had gone, Max said, "Now I have a pretty clear idea of what the possibility is with the Rockefeller Foundation, and the General Education Board is also contributing." He said, "I have to write a letter to Flexner to sum it all up." So he wrote a letter and showed it to me, and I said, "Max, you know him better than I do. I don't know him well. But this letter is too flattering." "Oh," Max said, "he's made that way. He'll like it." So he sent it. He got back a short note from Abe. It said, "Dear Mr. Mason. I've read your letter and want you to understand that the University of Chicago is not ours or mine, but *yours*."

Out of that, Max went ahead and created a new program consolidating Rush and bringing the full-time theory into use. He persuaded a great surgeon named Dallas Phemister to come over and be the first full-time man in medicine in the new clinics, in charge of surgery. That was Max's great educational contribution, consolidating the medical schools with science labs next door. Oh, he was a great president publicly. They loved him in Chicago. When he left, they had the headline across the Chicago *Tribune*, "Mason Quits University." They did think he was running away, and he was, for personal reasons, ready to move.

GARD: With this as background, then, could you describe how you first became involved with the General Education Board?

STEVENS: Arnett had been in the Foundation for some years on the General Education Board. It was in 1928 that Mason, who had worn out his welcome a little at Chicago, went to New York and met John D., Jr. John D. told Max he wanted him to be the next man in the Foundation, in charge of a new Division of Natural Science. As always in human nature and so in philanthropy, it seems, the first thing people think about is their own health. Well, the Foundation had had a strong program in public health, and under Vincent they brought Max Mason to head the new Division of Natural Science.

When he left, I stayed on with a man who had been a law school professor, and who then was vice-president. His name was Frederic Woodward. We ran the University in the best way we could for a year while they decided on Bob Hutchins as president. As one token afterwards I got a thousand dollars as a special addition to my salary. In those four years I made a friendship with Max, of course, and when Trevor Arnett went East, he asked me to be his vice-president of the General Education Board. So I had two friends in New York.

Up to that time two-thirds of the work of the Foundation, probably, was in public health and medicine, chiefly in the South under a remarkable man named Wickliffe Rose, who a little later became president of a new International Education Board. That operated continually until Rose retired. Well, Vincent went down as president of the Foundation, and Trevor Arnett was connected so strongly with John D., Jr. that Chicago had advanced their relations with Mr. Rockefeller Jr. personally, as well as with the Board members.

GARD: I wonder if we could clear up a couple of things here. One of the reasons why you went to the Rockefeller Foundation was that Mason had left the University of Chicago. You and another man had been running the University about a year, and at the end of that time Hutchins was brought in as president of the University. At that point you left. Now you had had one or two other offers, had you not?

STEVENS: Well, on the first of June, Hutchins came and had a wonderful reception. On, I guess about the first of July, walking to the Quadrangle Club to lunch with him, I said, "What's this idea of yours — that you're going to give the Bachelor's degree in two years? Why do you make every university and college in the country dislike you and us? Why don't you call it the New Chicago Degree?" "Oh, hell," he said, "the Bachelor's degree in America isn't worth anything anyway. So I don't care what they think." That was his pattern—to defy custom, and so to reform American education.

I immediately made up my mind, I don't care to go through this fight. Maybe I was wrong. I in many ways would have been happy to stay in Chicago, but I told him I was on the move. He offered me more salary and other things that weren't too tangible. He said, "This will always be a good place for you"; but I didn't work on that.

I let people know that I was looking for a move, and in three days I was offered three positions, one of which was this offer from Trevor Arnett to come as the vice-president of the General Education Board. Trevor, then, as president needed somebody who had been in education. He was a finance man. Having been told by everybody who knew anything about New York that you couldn't go there unless you had at least twenty-five or maybe fifty per cent more than you were getting at home, I held out until finally I got the ante up to 18,000 dollars, instead of the 10,000 dollars I was getting at Chicago. Trevor said, "That's all I can offer you." So that was my starting salary.

I went down for six weeks before I brought my family. I made the train trip ahead of my family in the company of George Vincent. He was about to end his term of duty as president of the Foundation.

GARD: Had you been in New York City before you made that initial train trip?

STEVENS: No.

GARD: What did you expect you would be getting into?

STEVENS: Oh, I knew a great deal about the Foundation. I had been in many discussions in Chicago with Foundation officers, talking to Max Mason in particular about getting grants. I knew what kind of outfit I was getting into, all right. As I said, some were old friends from our eighteen years at the University of Chicago — men taken into either the General Education Board or the Rockefeller Foundation as officers.

GARD: You really wanted the job.

STEVENS: Well, I wanted the money and I wanted to give my family a good break and also get out of the situation with Hutchins. Although I liked him very much, I was not particularly concerned then to start in on several years of struggle, which I knew were coming.

GARD: When you were making that train trip with Vincent, what were some of your thoughts concerning your new position with a philanthropic foundation?

STEVENS: I intended to intensify what I knew about the humanities and to help other people. That started, of course, with literature, classics, and finally the performing arts. We even got into radio and television, trying to reach the general public. I don't think there is much to say, except that I had been thoroughly schooled in what I was doing myself and I had helped operate a university for four years. I saw the humanities in relation to all the other disciplines.

GARD: How did your wife Ruth respond to this move?

STEVENS: It was her habit to "make no never mind" about a hurt, or to admit that a job was hard. When we moved a van of furniture from Chicago to our thirteen-room house in Montclair, New Jersey, I had Braxton, our Foundation messenger, come out on moving day to help out. He told me later, "Mrs. Stevens, she don't say 'Will you do it?' — she says, 'Come on, let's do it!'" I remember a typical example of her good humor. As we walked up Fifth Avenue to see the building where our Foundation office was soon to be, in order to help the Rockefellers fill the new but empty building in depression year 1933, Ruth looked to the top as I told her, "Up there is to be a fine restaurant." She answered, "Think of a little head of lettuce being carried way up there to be eaten!"

2. DYNAMIC BEGINNINGS OF THE HUMANITIES

I. General Education Board

GARD: You mentioned earlier that you made the train trip to New York with George Vincent. Could you add a few words about Vincent?

STEVENS: He was tall, lean, and agile, of clean-cut feature, always dressed in style. I had first known him as dean of the senior colleges, under President Judson; then he became known also as a remarkable

George Vincent

William Rainey Harper

Max Mason

David H. Stevens

Trevor Arnett

18

public speaker within the University and for city affairs as a speaker or toastmaster.

On the streets of Hyde Park, during my earlier years, I, like others, would be stopped at times by his father, retired Bishop Vincent of the Methodist church, with the question, "Do you know my son George?" This was a prelude to his informative but familiar remarks on his son, based on George's experience as part of the Chautauqua complex in New York State. George used to tell of the duties there: settling racial questions on use of the swimming pool or caring for great speakers. At a public address of a more formal sort, we would see his devoted father make marginal notes on the manuscript of audience reaction to the facts or stories.

George fully justified his reputation on the coming of Bob Hutchins in 1930. He was brought to be toastmaster at the elaborate dinner downtown, and his words were marked by a gatling-gun delivery of wisdom and witticism. Hutchins and Vincent possessed the backgrounds of life in two universities—Yale and Chicago—common ground for Vincent in his mingling of truth and fiction about academic life. Hutchins' address was equally lively, but delivered in more measured speech, with such true and pretended reminiscences of Yale as of his first day on the campus, when passing a store window that displayed women's lingerie he read the large sign set in a central position: "Welcome—Men of Yale!"

Hutchins later became a regular caller at our New York offices, always first paying his respects to John D., Jr. After one such "first stop"—this was in the late 1940's—he completed his calls on officers at the two boards on a lower floor of the RCA building and decided to have lunch with Raymond Fosdick and me. Fosdick was at that time president of the Foundation. As our elevator to the lunch room higher up stopped by chance to take on John D., Jr., Fosdick addressed the latter in his customary bantering style: "Oh, by the way, Mr. Rockefeller, Bob Hutchins has just been down in our offices and said that you sent him to ask for some money!" Surprise was registered on Mr. Rockefeller's face, and as he turned to Hutchins it was followed by a smile of silent interrogation. Bob's silence broke as we all got out, leaving Mr. Rockefeller to ride on up to his lunch room. Hutchins knew all of us sufficiently to relieve his embarrassment by a flood of adjectives and adverbs.

GARD: You've mentioned John D. Rockefeller, Jr. many times in your commentary; I wonder if you could say something about his appearance or what kind of personality he had.

STEVENS: He was small, precise in his dress, even-tempered, and he ran a meeting with a perfect handling of other people's points of view.

He had a tremendous sense of moral obligation, a sense of duty, perhaps through his father — I don't know — but he had it. He had a great sense of moral obligation, and with that, a self-effacement. He didn't want his part in a thing to be the determining factor or influence. To be sure, he had great influence in certain things they wanted to do or did do in New York City. He was a man who was most determined in moral matters, and this can be seen in the stories of how he brought up his boys, as when he sent Nelson through Dartmouth on 1500 dollars a year.

When I started work with the General Education Board, Arnett was running a Negro-white program in the South. I came in as his intellectual assistant. He was a finance man, a wonderful one. I was to develop a new General Education program. His program, with Jack Davis, and a number of Southerners who loved the Negro, was to keep the white and the blacks in balance, and not give the white any reason for resentment. That is what the General Education Board did in those days on the theory that if you did anything for the black you did it also for the white. So they had a very diverse program in public education and in college programs in all the southern states. I at once started in with him on what he wanted most to do, which was to continue the old Southern program.

I was not about to kick that bucket over. So I went along with him and just did my part, and finally we got along toward the period when the Progressive Education Association was going to disrupt all the old structure of secondary—and even college—education and let the student, as John Dewey said, "choose what he wanted to do by finding it." They are talking about this now in California, in the same language that Dewey used before. No intellectual discipline. We had a little belligerency, which I didn't show as much as I could.

GARD: In terms of your work with Arnett, then, you pretty much went along with him because of the situation at that time.

STEVENS: I protected him from what I might call pressures for experiment. That's what I did. Some people wanted to run loose with the program, with the unusual ideas of the progressive movement. Trevor and I just went along and did his old job. He had only three or four more years.

To start, Trevor took me on trips with his wife, and we covered the South, visiting all the Negro and white colleges, one right after the other, getting their budgets, and talking to their faculties to see who ought to be sent off for more training. I stayed one time with President Robert R. Moton of Tuskegee University. I lived in his university for two days. As we walked to the train, he said, "Here's where I leave you." Then he laughed, and he said, "I'll have a better bed than you, tonight. The Negro porters give me a compartment, but you'll sleep in a lower or an upper berth."

I know the old South pretty well, and particularly Atlanta, where there were three Negro colleges. One of them was the one where Ruth's mother had taught as a young girl. We got these colleges together and formed Atlanta University. There was a good deal of very interesting dickering on that proposition, because of course these colleges didn't rate each other as equals. One of them, which was the more powerful one, called Atlanta University, and the divinity school, called Clark, didn't think too much of Morehouse. I knew well the president of the fine woman's college, which John D., Jr. had started in memory of his mother, Spelman College for Women, which was on the campus with Atlanta. Over the hill a little way was Morehouse, and I remember a Spelman woman saying, "We don't want any of those Morehouse girls around our campus. Why, they even chew gum!"

Let me show you what a smart man Trevor Arnett was. He said, "All right, if you don't want them, we'll take care of them." He went across the city and bought a beautiful piece of land with General Education Board money, and that was to be the future home of Morehouse University. I remember when Trevor brought this up in the Board meeting. They laughed at him and said, "What are you up to?" "Well," he said, "you just let me go ahead. This is the way we've got to work. We have to build this thing, to get Morehouse on its feet." Well, this hadn't gone much further when the people in Atlanta University realized that they were building up an opponent in the Board; so they capitulated, and Morehouse was brought in, and a building built for them. Atlanta University emerged from that to become the universal center for black education.

GARD: What was he specifically going to do with this land? Was he bluffing?

STEVENS: It was a bluff, but if they had stayed militant, he would have gone ahead and got the money to put a college over there. But as soon as they saw that there was going to be an offshoot, then they gave in to Trevor and built a new building.

GARD: This is more or less Arnett's story. Did you have any workings in it at all?

STEVENS: Oh, yes. I went along with him all the time. That was a typical move of Trevor's. Toward the end of his time Trevor did another smart thing. He said, "You need a central library." Instead of having all five presidents' offices scattered around in these buildings, we'll put you all in this library." We had the president of Atlanta University Graduate School, the president of Atlanta, and the presidents of Clark and Morehouse. Spelman had its own campus. Trevor moved all their vaults to the basement of that building. The names are still on the doors, downstairs, and upstairs all had identical offices. That was it. So we got the complete consolidation with a very fine library, a good librarian, and a good purchasing program. They named it the Arnett Library, which made me very happy.

I used to watch Trevor operate. He was a very astute worker. He operated by telephone. He didn't write letters until he was ready to cinch something. He talked to people on the telephone, or he went out to see them.

GARD: Do you know how he first got associated with the Rockefeller Foundation?

STEVENS: Trevor had come from life in Minneapolis as bookkeeper in a railway office, where the paternal hand of Frederick Gates had found him for the University of Chicago business office. Trevor had risen to be comptroller of the University, and eventually he made pilgrimages to 26 Broadway with Father Goodspeed on money missions and so attracted the attention of John D., Jr.

Thomas Wakefield Goodspeed, who was the sacred saint of the old institution, was one of their wheelhorses to get that money. We have at the University a formal speech which Father Goodspeed wrote and memorized. He went to New York and recited it to John D., Jr. and Gates. Gates would interrupt him and say, "Well, you can't do that, you can't do that!" Father Goodspeed would let Gates talk; then he would start right in where he had stopped. He got his whole speech out, and he got the money. That's where Trevor knew the John D., Jr. and Gates pair.

Trevor was a short, fairly heavy-set Englishman, brought up in rural England, at Ludlow, where Ruth and I visited and met his brother and saw the old house where he was brought up. His brother, still a farmer, had the bacon hanging in the attic. Trevor, as a young boy, had been given the job of tax collector for the district. He was just a boy, working for his father, riding around on his horse, with saddlebags, collecting the money.

He was a very unusual man. He probably knew more about college finance before he got through than anybody else in his generation. When he was brought on as secretary of the Board, he went on a national tour with George Buttrick, examining private colleges to determine where the trustees would spread that first fifty million under a matching requirement toward endowment. They spent a year travelling all over the country. This must have been as early as 1920, somewhere in there.

GARD: This was not connected directly with the Negro colleges in the South?

STEVENS: No, this was the total development of the liberal, four-year colleges by distributing a mass of money to strengthen them. I wish they could do it again.

GARD: This was, in a sense, a movement into the humanities?

STEVENS: Yes, liberal education is where we belong. To resume about Buttrick. The best brief description of him was by Alan Gregg, who said he always tried for a lunch seat close enough to hear Buttrick talk. Of Arnett, one description is that he then (and to the end) used the same straight razor of his young years in Ludlow, England. He was a very lovable gentleman whose dream of this presidency of the General Education Board was made real by his friendship with John D., Jr. and their mutual devotion to the education of the black race. I have no doubt, for example, that creation of Laura Spelman College was because of the influence of Trevor Arnett and Buttrick.

There were exceptional things that had to occur in the Rockefeller Boards as a resulit of change in structure of such things as the International Education Board, which, when it went out of business, had certain formal obligations which the other boards of course backed up. For example, the commitment to create the 200-inch telescope, which is now on Mount Palomar in California, entailed a pledge and a payment due of what in all amounted to six million dollars.

How much of that the Board had to assume I don't know; but in one piece of odd luck in that story, when Trevor was out of the office, I had the chance, for the first and last time of my life, to sign a check for two million dollars. It had other general and heavy obligations which went on through the larger programs, such as we had with the Association of American Colleges, and part of it was to clear up the last large pledge to the Oriental Institute of the University of Chicago. That, of course, had been created largely by the Boards through the high regard for the work of James H. Breasted, as director of the program of archeological research in Egypt and later in what he called the "Great Circle," up through all of Asia Minor, where he worked the last part of his career. As a result of his work, he produced a most remarkable book on a basis useful to students and to readers, called *Ancient Times* (1916).

GARD: David, earlier you mentioned Jack Davis. Could you elaborate on his contribution to the Southern program?

STEVENS: Both Arnett and Buttrick relied on Jackson Davis. He *was* the Southern program of the General Education Board. Jack was the most knowing, most tactful of them all. He kept a balance between aid to white and black public education. In the college field he was equally active, and in the same style. As field man he had Leo M. Favrot, a Southerner who was familiar with all in southern state departments of education.

23

From Arnett, Davis gathered ideas and techniques of negotiation, but he gave more.

GARD: Did Arnett hire Davis?

STEVENS: I suppose so, although Davis had worked in the South with the Southern Education Board before he came to us. He had given his whole life to the South. He and Trevor grew up together in parallel parts of a total Negro-white program. He was a very good generalist and a very good classical scholar brought up with the old formula of what you would call classical backgrounds. Jackson Davis knew all the leaders of education, and public and political people in the South, and he really put the Southern plan for the Negro in working shape.

GARD: When you were vice-president of the General Education Board, did you ever make any attempts to strike out on your own in the humanities?

STEVENS: We started the drama and the Far Eastern programs with fellowships while I was in the General Education Board.

With its fixed traditions, the General Education Board was not to be disturbed by too much change of programs. The evident control of old policy by the old school ties and missionary spirit kept matters much as they had been. I got through some good, basic aids to public and college education with men like Lotus D. Coffman, president of the University of Minnesota, and two or three others. We accomplished much with the Association of American Colleges and the North Central Educational Association on national accrediting of colleges and university admission requirements, and on the quality of high-school work to gain admissions.

GARD: What was meant by the "old school ties and missionary spirit?" Why was the General Education Board not able to change?

STEVENS: Oh, it was able to change, but . . . . First of all, the General Education Board worked in the tradition that had been, what you would call, liberal education of the 1900's. They didn't try to change the subject matter of education. They went into teacher training, yes, but the chief thing was to keep the Negro college alive and to create it. To balance that, they spent their money on white schools and colleges equitably.

If you talk about old school ties, I don't know if you are referring to the old method or the fact of holding to Arnett's program until he retired. He wasn't to be disturbed, and I kept him from being disturbed too much. So we held to the old method of balancing white and Negro education all through the South, and nationally, doing something generally for the private college.

Also in those early years — around 1927 — had been established the first experiment in stimulating the humanities under the influence of such trustees as Jerome Green and Anson Phelps Stokes. After a general conference on what could be best done to dramatize their value in society, the General Education Board (partly under Flexner's advice, perhaps) made grants of five years each—considerable sums of money—to five universities, to carry on more general programs in the humanities. Princeton, Johns Hopkins, Chicago, Harvard, Yale — all had these large five-year grants.

This arbitrary selection was fruitful, but not based on national study. Each university played up its best projects. Yale was the only one that spent its money on developing younger men. The others all went in for large projects. At Princeton and Johns Hopkins, Edward Cooke Armstrong and Henry Carrington Lancaster worked on French literature in their periods of research; at Chicago it was John Manly's intensive study of Chaucer manuscripts; at Harvard, work was mainly in materials before 1600; and at Johns Hopkins, there was also a group editing Spenser for publication.

Yale made a wise use of its funds at a time when building up younger men was desired for the humanities' faculties, as well as the necessity to aid a few large editing projects. The humanities live in persons. To survive, replacements for all fields must be ready across the country at strategic points. With excellent presses Yale, Harvard, Chicago, and Berkeley were set to carry through in clear patterns. Stanford University, with the massive collections on the Far East and more in Russian subjects, had from us large amounts for men brought there to do basic research. Johns Hopkins is another example, as it developed from the start and specifically later in medicine under the guidance of Abe Flexner's brother, Simon, William H. Welch, and a few others. This desire for high-level and prompt production was also part of the reaction to a national study of medical schools, under Carnegie funds, which revealed the poor quality of work across the country except in the best locations.

GARD: How long did you work in the General Education Board?

STEVENS: I started with the General Education Board in 1930. I ran that job some years more after I took the Foundation job. I moved over into the Foundation in 1932. I didn't give up the General Education Board job until 1938, I think it was.

GARD: Was there any specific reason for that delay?

STEVENS: Well, we had to have continuity for Arnett, until he retired. By the time I had been in the Board office a couple of years as vice-president, I was then being pushed a little by Edmund Day, who had not been happy at not having been made president when George Vincent went out and Max was made president. Day told one of my best friends among the officers that he didn't think I was needed in that job and that he wanted it. He wanted not only to run Social Science but the General Education program. Alan Gregg, director for Medicine, a prince of a fellow, told me that. One of the trustees had told him. "Well," I said, "you go back and tell him that if they want my job they are welcome to it." And that was all I ever heard of that.

Toward the end of this time, as I was made director for Humanities, I was quite ready to give the job to a man who wanted it. So Day was brought in as director of Education under Trevor. The Progressive Education Association then dominated Day's thinking. He had a background of New England private school and university, with little idea of the national schemes for public education, and so he was ready for the outright progressivism of Washburne, Beatty, Rugg, and their master, John Dewey.

GARD: David, it might be a good idea to give a summary of the philosophy of progressive education at that time.

STEVENS: In my time, it was the growing art of freeing the student from dominant controls in the usual secondary school disciplines. It went on further into college to make the man more or less self-motivating and able to be freely expressive of all his feelings and thoughts. Schools were organized more on the basis of the individual, not on what you would call the disciplines or the intellectual control of tradition or the teacher.

It emphasized the importance of the individual, and as John Dewey pointed out, it was time this was done—not to have a simple a b c d e required, but to have the student show his own talents and have the teacher help the student expand his feelings and ideas rather than to tell him what to think. It sought to create the individual more in favor of the humanities than anything else, because it freed the individual to grow as he felt and believed.

GARD: There was some good and some bad to it, then?

STEVENS: Oh, yes.

GARD: And what was Edmund Day's relationship to progressive education?

STEVENS: He was a beginner. He had to learn. He was very flexible in dealing with the great body of men and women making up the Progressive Education Association, and he assisted them, naturally, more than the traditionalists. That's what he was devoted to. He was not a public school man at all; he was breaking his own tradition, going into the free air.

GARD: What was Day's relationship to Trevor Arnett?

STEVENS: He worked under Arnett. At one time we had a complete review of the current program of the Foundation with a most critical judgment of some parts at one of our Foundation Christmas meetings in Williamsburg. It was at this particular meeting that Day resented so much criticism of what he was trying to do that he leaned over and poked me and said, "Here's where I go out and get a job." It wasn't long before he was made president of Cornell University.

II. Rockefeller Foundation

GARD: You talked earlier about new directions in the humanities undertaken by the General Education Board. What was the Foundation itself doing in the humanities at this time?

STEVENS: During my years as vice-president of the General Education Board, the Foundation made two small moves into the humanities. One of them was at the insistence of the former secretary of the General Education Board, Abraham Flexner, who urged certain things that he thought would be desirable—in his style, trying to do massive things rather than building people. He encouraged Mr. Rockefeller in his archeological work, mainly by financing James H. Breasted of Chicago.

There is a good story about the ways of operation by Flexner and presumably why he was pensioned. He was not made president of the General Education Board as he had hoped nor given any continuing work when reorganization went on. He also wanted my work in Humanities. But he was given a pension and after that raised the money from the Bambergers for the Institute for Advanced Study at Princeton. Flexner was a lone worker, obsessed with the idea of "big things in a big way."

The other background story on humanities in years before my time concerns the University administration at Chicago and the work of Ed Capps. Edward Capps, a remarkable professor of Greek, had left Chicago with two other men—John Dewey and the head of Latin, George L. Hendricksen. The three of them went off as heads of departments at Columbia, Princeton, and Yale. This happened after two hundred professors signed a petition to the trustees, not to elect Judson president — Harry Pratt Judson — a good old Baptist who sat across the desk from Harper and according to Capps knew everything. They didn't know how they were going to get around him. These two hundred professors who signed the petition finally withered and gave up.

One little anecdote from an earlier time might be worth putting in. Ed Capps had stayed at Chicago for three or four summers, getting up the text of the massive series of decennial publications, a series of large research books, giving the record of the University in its first ten years. This was Harper's project to demonstrate the great and varied strength of his new University. So Capps stayed on there to satisfy Harper's demand that they get out these decennial publications, one for each area of study.

Ed gave up his vacations and also a chance to make money somewhere else. When he later left to go to Princeton, he asked to have full salary for his summers at the University Press. He was hard at work, teaching nine months of every year and working all summer for three years on this series. Capps said, as he was about to leave for Princeton, "Now look what I've done. I'm not going to take a two-thirds salary for those three or four summers." He thought he ought not to come under the rule of two-thirds pay if he took the money for a fourth quarter rather than the vacation. They said, "Yes, you are."

He had a considerable stake up in money; so Ed sent Dewey the word that he was in trouble. Capps got word from John Dewey, who said, "You get my lawyer in there, and he'll take care of it." And that's what the lawyer did. This lawyer from Chicago had a committee of the trustees meet him and Capps. He carried with him a copy of one of these volumes, and he said to the committee, "Here's a copy of the book." He opened the cover and said, "Well, look! What does it say? 'Prepared and Published at the order of the Trustees of the University.' Who the hell did you order? You ordered the head of the Press, of course." He said Ed wasn't here doing casual duty or trying to gather a lot of vacation credit. He was working for the good of the University. They gave Capps the money, and that's all there was to it.

The thing Ed Capps did for the Foundation was to start its Humanities program—as consultant before I came—from where he stood. He was a classicist. As American editor of the Loeb Classics, and in full-time teaching at Princeton, Ed would not — and could not — give attention to other than immediate opportunities in his own specialties. In this connection, I must add that he did his part to create the desire that the central district of Athens be bought in order to undertake the excavation of the Agora, ancient market place. Funds given by John D., Jr. (to a million dollars) enabled the American Classical School to carry through this great project. After our Division for Humanities erected the working museum for storage and for study, Mr. Rockefeller gave his second million to build again the Stoa of Attolus — full length of the east boundary of the excavation.

First the Rockefeller Foundation had Public Health; then Medicine under Pierce and next Alan Gregg. Their men were working abroad as well as all through this country, carrying on the work of the public health and medical programs. Warren Weaver came as head of Natural Sciences the same week as I was made director for Humanities. So we had five divisions: Public Health, Medicine, Natural Science, Social Science, and mine, the Humanities, which we started in 1932.

GARD: Max Mason, I think you said, went first to the Rockefeller Foundation as head of the Science Division.

STEVENS: That's all.

28

GARD: But he then became president. How long after he went there did he become president?

STEVENS: I don't know, whether it was days or weeks or months, but it was in the books. He knew it was.

GARD: Then it was Mason who established the Division for the Humanities?

STEVENS: Oh, yes. Plus pressures from Jerome Green and Anson Phelps Stokes, two trustees.

GARD: I just wanted to get this chronology straight. One other thing, David. Why were you picked as the director for Humanities?

STEVENS: I think Max trusted that I could do it, that's all. When I became director for Humanities in the Foundation, I was able to give all my time to the humanities instead of working in two boards.

GARD: So Max appointed you?

STEVENS: Well, the trustees did, but Max was the one who set up the new division.

GARD: When you became director for Humanities, how did you view what you were going to be doing?

STEVENS: I didn't worry about it. When I began my work as the director for Humanities, my viewpoint was that the long-range fundamentals of the humanities start with people — developing young, brilliant ones — and in starting programs that are not traditional, but needed.

GARD: Are you suggesting, then, that it was part of the basic philosophy of the Foundation that the older scholar is established already and has the means to go ahead with projects, whereas the young people with ideas, who do not have the influence, could be stifled?

STEVENS: That happens, of course; the other thing is the new fields of work that had to be opened up. The universities didn't have the money to do it and the men were not trained for it.

With that kind of program in mind, I started two things: one, to support steadily, every year, the American Council of Learned Societies, which was really a kept society of the Rockefeller Foundation from 1920 to 1950, when I left. As a declaration of independence, in the sense that the societies for the humanities were to be kept in a different relation to the Foundation on a modest subsidy, I gave them ten per cent of my budget every year to keep their office running. It was a budget that ran around a million dollars a year for regular work, apart from sums for larger projects like the Bodleian Library extension. Besides that, through a given society, or the Council, we gave funds every year for fellowships and for certain projects that we thought had to be moving.

The first field I energized, and I surely felt it important, was American literature and American language, and American studies generally.

It's an inconceivable fact today, perhaps, that when I went to New York I knew two men in American literature who really had national reputations. One was Percy Boynton of the University of Chicago, who taught general, and very strong undergraduate courses. The other was Curtis Hidden Page, formerly of Dartmouth, but then at Northwestern University, editor of the only useful text then on American poetry, in 1930. His *Chief American Poetry* came out in 1905.

Things were just about to break, as only between 1915 and 1930 had graduate training begun to loosen up for studies in American history, literature, language, and philosophy toward doctoral degrees. As a result, we began putting funds into fellowships for training young men in such overall basic projects as Spiller's three-volume cooperative history of American literature.

The second line of new endeavor was in the performing arts. Drama was alive at a few universities and in a few community playhouses. In 1930 these centers fostered original playwriting, training for teaching, and for performance; but no place was given performing arts in college or university budgets generally. The Foundation revived an organization named the National Theatre Conference, which had nourished these centers after Carnegie funding stopped. This came with the help of men like Brooks Atkinson and some of the playwrights, who gave us copyright releases of plays.

In a few years, with Rockefeller Foundation funds and the work of such leaders as Frederic McConnell, Barclay Leathem, Edward Mabie, Paul Green, and Alexander Drummond, the National Theatre Conference soon had a lively program of fellowships in all branches of theatre arts. We got an organization running that created prestige for drama not only in larger communities, but in colleges and universities. This organization went on during the war to produce training centers and to send men abroad to serve the armed forces, by directing and producing old and new stage plays. With the participation of such national leaders as Maxwell Anderson, Brooks Atkinson, and Barrett Clark, the development of a national theatre was fostered.

Over the years has come such national growth as appears in the eighty regional theatre houses (for music, drama, and dance) designed by George Izenour, one of its leading members. Also, the work of Hallie Flanagan, for the armed services and leaders sent abroad with our armies, demonstrated the national merit of the National Theatre Conference. In playwriting, the Conference did much, and its dedicated playreading member, Margo Jones, scanned hundreds of manuscripts while encouraging students on fellowships directly.

GARD: I want to get into the National Theatre Conference later on. I wonder if you could say something now about the structure of the American Council of Learned Societies as well as indicate the nature of some of the other programs you were able to initiate.

STEVENS: The ACLS began to operate in 1920, and their living budget came from us for twenty-five or thirty years. The ACLS was a living organization, but not much more in 1930. We supported it and gave it money for its projects, and it held annual meetings, had a staff, and turned out essential publications. The Foundation gave it basic help for survival and chances to develop new projects. They didn't get much philanthropy from anybody except us. The Carnegie Corporation gave them some money, and a few others. But they really depended on us. Now they depend on the Ford Foundation.

GARD: You gave them 100,000 dollars each year for operation?

STEVENS: Then we gave them projects up to two or three hundred thousand, which is small money today. But it was good money in those days. And we drove bargains everywhere for people who wanted help. For example, if I talked to you, I would say, "How much can you give toward this project? At the end of five years, will you take it over completely?" That's the way we went into them. You never get tied up.

GARD: When you gave that 100,000 dollars to the ACLS, did you have any control over the money?

STEVENS: They operated on their own, and they were very careful not to get off our payroll. I tried to tell them once, "You need fifty thousand a year to run your office. I'll go to the Foundation and ask for a million dollars endowment." They didn't want to do that. They didn't want to take a chance of being turned loose. I don't know how vital the ACLS is today. They have a good man now, Robert M. Lumiansky, who lately went in as president.

GARD: What were some of the large grants you made in the humanities? You mentioned the Bodleian Library extension.

STEVENS: Large grants for single projects went to the extension of the Bodleian at Oxford University (two and one-half millions); to library projects, in Europe for filming source materials for American history; to international library projects giving source materials for advanced research in the United States and Western Europe; for the Far East and Russia for book stocks needed by Foundation fellows; and for the language research and training centers of Harvard, Columbia, Chicago, Yale, California at Berkeley, the Library of Congress, and elsewhere.

Eugene B. Power

Edward F. D'Arms

Mortimer Graves

Robert E. Spiller

J. Frank Dobie

Paul Green

Samuel Selden

Josephina Niggli

George C. Izenour

John W. Parker

Part Two
Men and Ideas

3. SCHOLARS AND UNIVERSITIES

I. Libraries and Scholars in Mexico

STEVENS: All of these things that I have mentioned had relevance, as did the output from work in drama, to the war effort; and from 1933 to 1950, these new growths were built into the American resources for humanities. I could carry on in more detail about the work in libraries, American studies, in drama, and foreign commitments in several areas for international meanings in the humanities.

GARD: You might just as well go right on with it.

STEVENS: Well, let's begin with the American Library Association. It sounds a little stuffy, perhaps, to people not deeply involved in creating new fields of research, teaching, and production. All the young men and women needed for future growth! We began on the assumption that the humanities exist in the individual and for the individual, to make constant the understanding of the traditions of culture in all known history. That required that we get into the hands of the scholars the books, or the copies of the books, that they needed in order to make progress in research and reduce the waste of effort and the time for taking degrees.

One of our most unusual things in library work was in Mexico City. The American Library Association, with Harry Lydenberg, who had retired as librarian of the New York Public Library (headquarters at forty-second street), as operator, worked up a program to establish in Mexico City the first public library south of the United States. It's hard to believe that's true. With our money we rented a fine building on the Reforma, one of the big streets in the center of town. It was a three-story building. Lydenberg went down and organized collections and bought extensively, of course.

The first floor was the first public reading room ever opened in Latin America. It had newspapers and open-shelved books. The second floor was the shelf distribution for adults. The third floor was the children's collection. They would draw their books out. When I was there one day, I saw all these little kids screaming and running up the stairs like mice, and down again with new books. I suppose the original collection of three thousand books in Spanish, and the same number in English, went out at least once a week. The whole collection. These kids just stirred those books up and moved them. The thing was a great success from the beginning.

One of the greatest tributes I think we ever had in the Foundation in my field was the incidental one from Ed Murrow in a long article about Mexico. He told about talking with a diplomat in Mexican service who said, "Of all the things the Foundation has done in Mexico and for Mexico, starting that public library was the most important." Out of it came a demand on the Mexican government to start a series of provincial libraries, and this was imitated by other states of Latin America. It all started to open the public mind to where it would never again believe in arbitrary control by church or state as permissible.

We had a committee there, composed of Mexicans and Americans, running that library. One of the men was a dispossessed Spanish landlord who had great holdings that the government had taken from him. He was a man of great intellectual interest who also had a sense of humor. He became vice-president of a bank in the center of Mexico City.

One day I was up in the mezzanine floor, where he had his desk, when we looked down at the front door and saw Lydenberg coming in. He came upstairs and sat down beside us, and our Spanish-Mexican asked him, "Well, how's everything?" "Oh," he said, "it's terrible. I've got to make a bad confession. They broke into my library last night and stole all the toilet seats." Our friend laughed and slapped him on the knee and said, "Now—you are a real Mexican!" Well, that wasn't an unusual incident, because a common story was that if a new building was opened, a man would come looking for an apartment and keep looking at them until he got to the top floor. Meanwhile, an accomplice would come below, floor by floor, and if the water had not been turned on, would steal all the faucets.

I could tell you a great deal about the poverty in Mexico. The worst example I ever saw was on a night when I was going home. I saw a very bedraggled old man going along the big billboards, with bags, pulling out pieces of loose paper that he would take off to sell for a penny or two.

The public library for all, that we had in Mexico City, was paralleled by one at the other end of the scale in Mexico. The Spanish government had dispossessed all the Jewish scholars, or rather, all the liberals—not only Jewish—but all professors who were not in favor of the government after the unsuccessful rebellion. We did a great deal in Mexico and a considerable amount in history, language, and philosophy in all of Latin America, by finally centering it in the school created by the Mexican government, to take care of these exiled liberals, the Colegio de México. That turned out to be a magnificent investment of not very much money.

GARD: Do you remember some of the individuals who were involved in this project?

STEVENS: This project was under two or three famous scholars of Mexico. The greatest one for varied abilities undoubtedly was Alfonso Reyes. Another man, Cosio Villegas, in history, was first in all of South America.

This research center had humanists in literature, language, and history, and with money from the Mexican government they were given opportunity not only to go on with their studies but to publish. This was a most remarkable break for sustained scholarly activity in Mexico, because before that Reyes and Villegas and a few others were solitary scholars. Reyes was also a diplomat and a great public figure as critic and a poet. Now they had a nucleus of scholars, and new books began to appear, all under the imprint of the government and paid for by the government.

There was this one story about Cosio Villegas. He said to me, "I know more people of influence here than others, and I have family prestige in Mexico; so I'm safe compared to any other historian. If this sounds egotistical, you may ask anybody today in Mexico and hear what they say. But you don't need to, because I can tell you that I'm the only man in Mexico who could write an honest, unbiased history of Mexico since the revolution and be let alone." Well, we got the money for Villegas and he fully justified our confidence. His books are classics.

Reyes established a school of history and literary criticism. Then we began to import men from other parts of Latin America. After a visit to Buenos Aires, I brought up one of the great language specialists and one of his subordinates to start studies in Portuguese and Spanish that would produce not only scholarly men and needed works, but critical studies of the history of language that would lead to the scientific production of textbooks and dictionaries. One young man named Leopoldo Zea turned out to be a prodigious scholar. He now is one of the older and best men in the group.

Apart from these men we had helped another strong leader in Mexico City named Alfonso Caso, who, like Cosio Villegas and Reyes, was an individualist so strong in his relationships with the government and of such ability that no one would touch him. He was for a generation in charge of all excavation in Mexico and of all the museums. We gave him a great deal of help, not in archeological excavation, but in historical studies and in fellowships for his younger men.

In the midst of this program he came to New York City and in the old Pennsylvania Station had a magnificent exhibit of things found in his excavations, particularly at Mount Alban. There were the most precious gold and silver objects, many of them showing very definitely a relationship, it seemed to me, with Egypt, in design and variety. That's where I first got very well acquainted with him.

Some time later we had him at the University of Chicago for a summer course, which ought to be mentioned, because it showed the quality of the man. I came out one day to see him at the University. He just handed me a telegram from one of his friends in Mexico City saying,

"Come home right away, they're trying to take your posts under the government away from you." He said, "Here's the answer I sent them: 'I signed a contract to stay here until the 15th of August. Then I'll come home.'" They never got the better of Alfonso Caso. He went on securely through his whole life and created that magnificent archeological museum at Chapultepec, which is probably the finest of its kind in the world, with specimens and a detailed explanation of the whole course of archeological evidence from the Mayan period and all the other phases of Mexican history.

There still are other things in Mexico that we could have helped, but our program had little to do with art, except indirectly. There was a very unusual man named René d'Harnoncourt, who belonged to a titled family in Austria but who had lost contact with his family and had lost his money. He turned up in Mexico in golf trousers and wearing a derby hat! He was a six foot two-inch man who was steeped in the meanings of history and art. He was a magnificent person as well as a scholar, and he did enough with the leaders in Mexico that they will remember him always.

When he came back to Mexico from the Museum of Modern Art, where he had become director, he brought into being the first really modern exhibition of objects in museum style, in cooperation with famous Mexican artists, who with the help of René d'Harnoncourt produced a great many fine books on Mexican art. These artists, with René, then, went to work creating a tradition of museum exhibition and setting up exceptional exhibitions of art in Mexico City. In this way they created the background of what became part of the work of Alfonso Caso. Well, René went on with those contacts, with some of our help, to do a great deal for Mexican art by developing young people. But his great contribution was in museum-exhibition techniques.

The Mexican natives and Spanish expatriates have published extraordinary books on language, history, literature, and Mexican art. The Foundation, of course, had been in Mexico for twenty-five years in public health. For example, we had spent nine million dollars in eradicating foot-and-mouth disease, brought in when some rich Mexicans imported Brahman bulls. These men broke the law that required any animal brought in to be isolated for three months. They brought foot-and-mouth disease from Argentina, but our government stamped it out. We sent teams of men in to find the animals and destroy them and pay the farmers.

One small thing that grew up in Mexico, generally through contact with American linguists, was native work in the study of Mexican dialects and writing of texts on both history and language, which were used for school texts. I remember I went out into the country on one of the hottest days of my life, walking through a cornfield to find an American scholar, Morris Swadesh, who had gone out there to live with the natives and record native dialects in order to help them write their own books in their own language.

II. The Development of Microfilm

Now, aside from the libraries for popular use throughout Latin America, similar to the one I told you about in Mexico City, we had a massive job in library work in producing in later years a total reproduction in volume form of the Library of Congress catalog. This was given, I think, to some thirty or forty libraries abroad—not that they would buy the old or new books—but so they would know the books existed and could secure film copies. They could send over and get copies of articles and books, and of special titles in any field. In other words, the catalog of the Library of Congress, which we reproduced for world-wide gifts after the end of the Second World War, carried the basis of good scholarship into every part of the world.

I recall when we started doing something really fundamental in the library field to get the resources that the humanists must have in their hands when they were writing a book or scholarly article. Carnegie Corporation had done substantial things, very substantial in several ways in the higher education area, but not nearly enough to help the humanists. So Henry Lydenberg, of the New York Public Library, was one of the men we came in constant contact with working up projects. He was a very remarkable fellow, as I think I may have already noted, and I could name several others. One of them was a man at the Library of Congress, Herbert Putnam, who was director. We found a quick process of growth into this field through the opportunity of microfilm, with the help of an imaginative and dedicated individual named Eugene Power, who had conceived of microfilm as a medium for supplying copies of rare books to American libraries. Eventually, there was developed a small microfilm reading machine for libraries. It was at this point that Power and I came into contact with the Eastman Kodak Company. I had already secured money for Power to work in Europe with two or three instruments, as well as for men to be working with him around the clock, getting copies of American documents on our history and literature so they could be stored in American libraries.

Power said, "We've got to get reading machines into libraries and get them produced and sold as a marketable product, to carry this idea all through the library world." So he took me along down to Eastman. Well, they had one newspaper camera which could take a page of a newspaper and reproduce it somewhat reduced. We told Eastman what we were going to do in Europe, on bringing these documents in and starting readers on the use of microfilm—not the large size—but small copies on 35 mm film as well, which could be enlarged with the reading machines. So for the next step you could copy a whole newspaper or a whole book and put it away in a little case. That's very commonplace today. Well, the Eastman specialists were very timid about it, and for a commercial firm, I thought they were very dull, or at least cautious, with Power.

There was another man besides Power who was very important in print copying, named Rupert H. Draeger. He was a captain in the United States Navy, who on his long sea journeys had developed a little shop in his ship where he worked on making the first photographic machine that could do what we wanted. It would copy newspapers but also make small copies which could then be enlarged and read on a reading machine. We didn't have the reading machine; we had Draeger's original machine which he had built in Peking, where he was on duty, and we had another one, which he had built in the United States.

Well, Draeger was evicted from China at the time of the Japanese invasion and came to the United States; so we had his help along with Power's to try to break into this new field. As we got into it further, and Draeger and Power were ready to exploit their new opportunities, we financed a running exhibit at the World's Fair Exposition in Paris in 1937, where we set up a Draeger camera and an Eastman camera and ran them constantly, showing people — especially librarians — how the process worked. We made copies of rare books and documents for the Bibliothèque Nationale in Paris.

GARD: This exhibition must have been essential in promoting the use of microfilm throughout the world.

STEVENS: Oh, yes. Those two men, Draeger and Power, had the help of a very unusual young man from the University of Chicago named Herman Fussler, then a librarian of the University, and an odd little man named M. Llewellyn Raney, who was head librarian. Raney and Fussler became not only pioneers as demonstrators in Paris but in starting copying centers elsewhere in the United States as well. With their help we got a program started of creating centers of photography for microfilm, in Chicago, at forty-second street in New York City, and the Library of Congress. After the war we had a complete laboratory in the British Museum and a floating one in Europe, gathering material, all of which was deposited and is now available to anybody, at the Library of Congress.

In all of these places we financed the buying of the cameras and readers by substantial subsidies. I think Draeger built three of them. By that time the Eastman people had waked up and were starting to produce more microfilm cameras as well as more reading machines of good quality. Then the inventive skill of Mr. Power began to produce a portable, reasonably priced reading machine, and in a little while there were a great many in use. Today it's the basis of all copying and has been refined so that now they can put a whole book on a few pieces of cardboard the size of a library card, and you can put a whole library in a very small scale on film rolls to be available for research work. Microfilm, I think, is the most unusual thing that, with the help of Eugene Power and Herman Fussler and Raney and Draeger, we were able to put into the library service of the world.

Then a microfilm institute was created which had annual meetings and stimulated educational use and trade use of the service. And it wasn't very long until microfilm was a national asset in industry and in business as well as in education. Now we have reached the point where all the publishers and university presses are really concerned over a bill in Congress that is intended to restrict the use of copying machines. People in education, business, and industry are not only copying articles and storing them in their libraries or laboratories for reference and research, they are beginning to copy whole books — which of course very soon gets to be an infringement of the copyright act. So there is a serious national study going on now. All the university libraries, business, industry, and particularly the publishing houses are greatly concerned with what this act is to contain.

EUGENE B. POWER: Although I had known him earlier, my first close contact with David Stevens came about 1940. Dr. Waldo Leland, secretary of the American Council of Learned Societies (ACLS) had talked to David Stevens about the possibilities of microfilming materials in foreign archives which were in danger from bombing and needed by American scholars. This followed fairly closely on the path of Robert Binkley, who had been chairman of the Joint Committee on Materials for Research, indirectly supported by the Rockefeller Foundation. This was sponsored by both the ACLS and the Social Science Research Council.

There was great interest in the developing technique of microfilm at that time and it was felt that this might be the medium which could be used to bring the desired material to the United States.

A conference was called on 5 and 6 June, 1940, at the Library of Congress, by the ACLS. After much discussion, it was agreed that efforts would be made to microfilm those portions of British archives which could be made available for this purpose. David Stevens gave an initial grant to the ACLS of $30,000.00 for this purpose, the funds to be administered by the Library of Congress. My firm, University Microfilms, was given the responsibility of doing the actual microfilming. Because of the unusual good fortune we had in doing this work in various emergency depositories in England, the grant was later increased to $140,000.00 and the work was carried on during the war. At the conclusion, we had filmed about six million pages of valuable manuscript material and the negatives were placed in the Library of Congress.

There were other grants from Rockefeller and from Carnegie, but I cannot at this time remember which was which. However, I do know that David Stevens was always interested in the promise which microfilm had as an aid to scholarship and as a means of supplementing the holdings of American libraries. I know that his services to American scholarship were very great indeed at a time when the humanities were a poor stepchild of the sources of funding.

STEVENS: Of all copying done in Europe to bring home copies of documents (thousands of them) for use of our own scholars, that in the British Museum was foremost. The British Museum is one of the three depositories for everything published in Great Britain, but their idea of cataloguing was very primitive. All our scholars working in Great Britain were being handicapped, especially the humanists, by the length of time it took to get a book. They had the books all right, but the cataloguing was either poor or nonexistent.

GARD: If you went to find something, how did you do it?

STEVENS: You looked for it in one of scores of index books. If the title wasn't pasted up, you didn't know that it was in the library. You couldn't get it. This lack of good catalogues of the total holdings, and, for those titles listed in their clumsy pasted-slip volumes, gave slow service of only a limited number at a time to readers. There was no real guide to total holdings, and it was long in arrears. It was part of our entry into the Bodleian program to start a project which would yield quick resource by card catalog to what existed.

GARD: How were you able to use the microfilm idea in this case?

STEVENS: We financed an experimental demonstration there with microfilm—old-style photostats, at first, then microfilms for reading machines—which could be used by any library or individual. These were made on the Museum premises. We got a lot of copied materials out of the British Museum for the Library of Congress, just as we did in China. Before the war wrecked everything, we brought out a lot of copies of rare manuscripts from the National Library of Peking.

But to go back to the catalog situation. We went to the British Museum. Professor Manly was there working on his Chaucer project, and he and I talked to the secretary of the Museum, Arundell J. Esdaile. We rarely then made a grant of more than five years; and although I didn't have complete authority to do so, I tried, in this case, for the British Museum catalog. I asked if they would take a ten-year grant, of considerable money, to push the cataloguing on a modern scale, instead of doing what they did do, to get out cards rapidly and produce something that could be easily read. Well, the British answer that I got was no, they wouldn't get into it, because they would then have developed a group of men who at the end of ten years would demand, or probably demand, pensions and work. Their conservatism kept them motionless. Aid to research use of that storehouse is still probably sorely needed, but can come only from outside under current conditions. The greatest storehouse of old cultural values in the Western world is partly closed.

So we started with another unit in Great Britain called the National Library, which had its headquarters near the British Museum. It operated for the whole country on a catch-as-catch-can basis, as a clearing house for the loan of books among the universities and the big libraries. They had a big stock of books, which they would loan out on requisition. We got them started in producing a national catalog index of books covering the outlying universities and public libraries so all could locate rare items and borrow them. That was very fruitful.

We even went so far as to train some "American-type" librarians, by shipping over a few men who would then go back and be teachers of library science. We brought over one creative man who lived two years in the States and went back to do valuable work. I think they probably are operating still on that scale, working to produce a national network of loan privilege outside of the big British Museum.

The American Library Association became one of the finest agents through which resources were developed for the humanist. One thing done was to help the Association erect a new and unique building at the University of Chicago and thus create a central depository where thirteen of the major universities and colleges who became subscribers to this service would send duplicate copies of books they didn't need, or in some cases, unusual items they wouldn't need except by requisition occasionally.

This was done with our money, to be sure, but the control of the center was in the hands of a committee directed by Herman Fussler. Fussler was in charge of the collecting and servicing of calls from these institutions asking for information or for copies of books given by many of these libraries. They built this center with very little aisle space and with solid book stacks, in which you could pull out a shelf on rollers; so there was at least fifty per cent more storage space in the same building. It has operated on a permanent basis with a modest budget produced by this network of midwestern libraries.

Our other work in connection with libraries in the United States had such an unusual purpose as starting distribution abroad, after the war, of scholarly and scientific journals. When foreign nations lost their runs of journals in all fields, we set up a rather courageous operation in 1946 under a woman, Alice Dulany Ball, who was just indomitable. She took this almost impossible job, and advertised all over the country, saying, you don't want your old journal files. You've got them in the library. Give them to us. She got large floor space in the Library of Congress, to which all professors in our universities in the humanities (and some in science) sent their spare copies of journals—tons of these—to be classified, tied up, and shipped steadily, at Federal cost, to centers all over Europe. The government and the Smithsonian took over shipping costs, and later on all salaries. These universities in Europe had had no journals during the war. It put these universities on their feet. I think she is still doing this, an international educational philanthropy.

The history of the Library of Congress collection in Chinese is very extraordinary. That was an example of how things grow and spread from a single act. Teddy Roosevelt was the man who started the Library of Congress in Chinese. There was a wealthy nobleman in Eastern Russia who sent a letter to the Library of Congress, saying, as was customary in Russia, that as he came near the end of life, he wished to give his library to a Russian institution. But his family needed the money, and he had this ancestral collection of basic Chinese titles, properly bound, which he wanted to sell.

Teddy Roosevelt, who was quite a novice at such things, but who had a great deal of audacity, got a large appropriation through Congress to buy that library. The Library of Congress thus became one of the best foreign centers for study in Chinese in the world. (There was one in Paris, another in Leyden, another in Germany.) From that point we went on feeding new titles into the collection at the Library of Congress, making that a place for the work of scholars from our universities and abroad. As the Japanese armies invaded China and shortly took over everything, the national librarian got rare manuscripts — a great many titles — out to Shanghai, and with our money we brought them over to put them in the Library of Congress as a gift from the former national Chinese government.

That is another haul of great value that has made America one of the finest centers for work in Chinese in the world. Of course, that is partly due to the fact that we have a fine library system and a body of trained scholars who are bringing up a new generation and training not only humanists, but scientists, social scientists, and businessmen in Chinese.

III.   Creating New Dictionaries

STEVENS: Bob, if you want a few incidental background pictures of what a foundation can do, how it can relate prominent people to the work of the university world, or the presses, or the libraries of the world, I can give you many examples.

University presses, in my day, became quite remarkable in their influence, following the leads of Harvard and Chicago. Take as an example the press of the University of North Carolina, where there was an extraordinary staff of men in social studies. That press probably had more influence in the South than any other part of the university system, because of the men it trained and the books it published on basic problems of the South. That was one of the presses that the Foundation aided. It gave them basic money, not to do their field work, but to bring out books that the University would want to bring out, but could not afford to.

We didn't try to make still stronger the big presses, like Harvard, Yale, and Chicago, by general subsidies. We gave to minor presses, as at North Carolina, Oklahoma, and to places where we had special fields of interest, as in Chinese studies and for the dictionaries and texts in unusual demand for the war. These were programs for getting the humanities into action where they were useful. In 1930 the need was very great for extra money to bring scholarly manuscripts to print. They didn't have any loose money in those days.

And that's right where they are now. The story came out recently in the newspapers that six hundred thousand dollars has just been secured for a committee under the editor of the press at Yale, Chester Kerr. The money is to be spent to determine a publishing policy for scholarly and trade books. So the funds are provided to gather data that will be to the advantage of the university presses as well as to the commercial publishers. On the legal side of the matter, the need to protect the copyright for the author and for the publisher is another important problem that is being addressed by this committee.

I know that three years of study are to be basic and probably in the end very fruitful. But it's a job that is not treated at all like an emergency, which it is. The whole story is that at the moment the small presses are dying—they're closing down. Maybe some of the medium-sized ones will be in trouble. Certainly the great ones, like Harvard and Chicago, and half a dozen others, will be badly hampered. I don't know how astute this committee will be, or how much can be gained through the National Endowment for the Humanities, but it would be a great help to the humanistic scholar if we had more assurance that whatever he did would someday come into print.

It is quite as important that funds be provided for publishing in the humanities as it is for the Endowment for the Arts to look after the symphonies in the country. Think of what 25,000 dollars a year, promised to recur for ten years, would do if given to eight or ten or fifteen of the strong presses that are gradually now being shut down or cut down by lack of funds. That would be the right kind of commitment, it seems to me, for the Endowment for the Humanities to make.

I think the presses are in much more danger of crippling trouble than any other part of our university system, except the libraries. Care of buildings and grounds in universities and new buildings are easier to get money for, as for the sciences and medicine, than either the social sciences or the humanities. It's not an uncommon administrative decision that "we must get a hundred thousand out of this budget. Let's take fifty thousand from the library items and this year let the university press get along."

I told you a story or two about the early days of the University of Chicago Press and of their creation of journals, and how the Library of Congress even now helps supply the journal market abroad. Those are the things that somebody has first to start and next maintain as national requirements for intellectual security and for growth in all fields of learning. No other living nation has equal responsibility to all others. Our eminence in sources of knowledge and for world service to scholars is America's true place of world leadership—not for weapons, or, today, in financial security for foreign countries under subsidy.

Sometimes a task is beyond the reach of the universities and at times even impractical as a commercial project. So a foundation must carry both burdens, and particularly in opening new fields—as in wartime—or under severe economic setbacks. I might run over a few of the great tasks of the humanities that are being done by foresighted training of personnel, and note how important it is to keep these projects alive, so that men and materials can develop the great resources of all human culture.

As an example, take the business of revising existing dictionaries and producing entirely new ones. An English professor, William Allan Neilson, brought out the Merriam Webster's second edition in 1934. Tom Knott worked for them ten years, at a moderately good salary for a professor in those days. You can't imagine the millions of dollars that went into that project. Now the third edition is out, and that again took a great, slow-return investment, just as the *Encyclopedia Britannica* did for its last edition. Scholars are wanted for such projects, and they are primarily to be found in universities.

Years ago, the British started a project to show the history of English words. By using a vast number of readers all over the English-speaking world, representative books were scanned to gather meanings of words as they were found from their earliest usage up to the time the *Oxford English Dictionary* was printed. The aim was to get a "biography of a word" out of usage in every generation of its use. The *Oxford English Dictionary* was launched back before the eighties—I don't know the date. The fact that they would start this shows the kind of courage the British have in their scholarship. It went on under the head of a general editor who finally was retired. One of his assistants, William A. Craigie, a Scotchman, became the general editor. Craigie carried the *Oxford English Dictionary* through to completion and the printing of it. Then they made a supplement of the words that had emerged since the first book came out, so that in the long run Craigie was the one who mastered the completion of the *Oxford English Dictionary* in England.

Then Manly, at Chicago, saw the fact of the need of an American supplement, because we have a vocabulary that is different from the British and have evolved a great many original words, and a great many changes in meaning of words. He persuaded the University to bring Craigie over, and on some of this five-year grant money started Craigie on getting readers all over the world, particularly in England and America, making slips carrying examples of usage. As the slips came in, all were filed under their alphabetic places.

Craigie ran that job through to a finish and brought out a three-volume *Dictionary of American English* with the aid of Mitford M. Mathews, who became the inheritor of all of Craigie's contacts and systems. He is now the outstanding lexicographer in the United States. He is consulted by the makers of dictionaries and consulted by scholars. The *Dictionary of American English,* completed at the University of Chicago, printed at its Press, has become a world asset in the field of language.

There was one other dictionary that I had a good deal of interest in. During the war we had armies, of course, going into Korea, and at that time there were only two men, sons of a missionary family, working at the University of California, who knew Korean by oral experience. They became wartime workers in Korean and then became, under some aid from us, specialists in training other people. That was the beginning of what I hope is to be a small nucleus of scholarship in Korean studies that will never die out.

But the one I'm talking of is a dictionary that came out of Korea itself. When the Japanese went into Korea and conquered it, they tried to destroy Korean culture and make Korea a Japanese province. But during all those years of Japanese occupation and national enslavement, the old scholars of Korea were working on gathering examples, just the way it was done for the two I've mentioned, the *Oxford* and the *American* dictionaries. During the Japanese occupation these scholars, working secretly, took different books, wrote out word meanings, and thus got during all these years of secret work a great mass of cards and slips out of which could be created the first Korean-Korean dictionary.

As Korea became a free nation, our government had men working in Korea—mostly under Army money, none of them under our money—on reestablishing the educational system. The scholars had this collection of material to make the first Korean dictionary, but they had no money. They had no means to bring it about, and no one to open up print shops. So they came to us, and with the help of the Navy, we got together a complete body of essential material to produce a five-volume dictionary of the Korean language. They told us about what it would be in cost. We got the string, the glue, the boards, the paper, the ink—everything to produce a printing shop product—and put it on a Navy ship just before it left for Korea. Korean printers produced the five-volume Korean dictionary, which is now the basis for Korean education. Now they have the material to produce schoolbooks, to get people to write original material, and to get books and newspapers printed. They had a wonderful start and made the most of it.

I have one very pleasant personal fact in regard to this opening up of Korea as a culture after the Japanese and Chinese evacuation. The United States government was on the job trying to provide materials to help their educational institutions. I had written a book called *The Changing Humanities,* out in 1953, reviewing all the various types of active humanistic work as I saw it and as it was going to develop. It was a good-sized book that went out of print rather rapidly. Without my knowing, the government got a young Korean to translate it into Korean and gave away five thousand copies in Korea. All I got out of it was five free copies, but I didn't mind. I was delighted to have had a chance like that.

We have neglected many opportunities in this country for such major gifts for national service. Compared to Great Britain, we are rather dilatory. For instance, some years ago Adolph S. Ochs, editor and owner of the *New York Times,* gave the American Council of Learned Societies five hundred thousand dollars to start a *Dictionary of American Biography.* We didn't have anything else then but the commercial *Who's Who in America.* The Council set a small staff to work and finally got out twenty volumes and an index volume, using the funds given by Mr. Ochs. With that they had a commitment to go on working. The Rockefeller Foundation gave money to keep the project alive, and meanwhile they worked out what they called a trade agreement with Scribner's to print supplements to the old edition. I think the ACLS gets a small royalty.

But Scribner's keeps up the marketing and now is slowly, with the help of the ACLS, developing texts for regular supplements.

Since issuing the first twenty volumes, they have done three volumes, each volume covering a five-year period. Editors select for study a list of notable Americans who have died in a five-year period. They put researchers to work to dig up the facts and write the text. To date, the three volumes that have been brought out cover only the years to 1945. The last volume came out last November, and they promise a fourth supplement some time next spring.* But notice the fact of the date. This third volume, brought out in November, 1973, leaves a gap of nearly thirty years that has to be covered, a good part of it to be prepared after the contemporaries of these men are dead, and perhaps their papers scattered.

Many of the people who today, like me, could give information, died before they got the chance. When John Manly died, there were twenty people who could have told unusual stories about him. That's all lost. The only inner resources they have today on some of these men is what Columbia University did, with the help of Allan Nevins, to make oral history an established part of their operating university program. They call in notable men and women and have them answer questions, and all of this is recorded on tape. So stored away at Columbia is a stack of material on a selected few.

I don't suppose that there is any greater hope that I have than that the newly-endowed—or rather, financed—Endowment for the Humanities, under Federal money, will get down to such basic things and not try to give so many fellowships where fields are fairly well cared for by the universities and the American Council of Learned Societies. Instead, this Endowment should get into some of the big things that nobody else will do and which are permanent aids to all people, such as steady finance for the *Dictionary of American Biography*. But publication timing and scholarly control of source materials are against fine quality in biographic accounting for American leaders of yesterday. This *Dictionary of American Biography* has an isolated editor, and I don't know his staff. Many of their recent sketches are thin, and there are many errors in the choice of names.

Meanwhile the British got stirred up over their own dictionary—the *Dictionary of National Biography* — the *DNB,* which was launched and seen through its first fifty years by Sir Leslie Stephen. About the time we were talking about this American dictionary, and Mr. Ochs was getting it launched with a few older scholars here, the British went at their

---

*Supplement Four, covering the years 1946-1950, was published in 1974.

job. Well, they didn't have money, they didn't have the wealth of scholarship, or the number of people available — but what did they do? They got that whole *DNB* brought down to date, and today it's available in any good library in a brand-new uniform edition, finely edited—a great tool for any student of any personal history or of British institutions. We are very lax not to do more on such massive projects in the national interest and less on 1976 bicentennial public display.

Another project just like that, only of much lower interest generally, but very important for the history of culture, is on at the University of Chicago, where for forty years they have been developing from great stores of material an Assyrian dictionary. It is something that none but a university faculty, backed by constant financing, will ever finish. I wish we could get the National Endowment for the Humanities to put money into things like libraries and presses and such major projects as dictionaries, which are not commercial, but absolutely fundamental to the world of knowledge.

I have one other dictionary in mind that we had a lot to do with. A devoted scholar named John K. Birge, who was a missionary in Turkey, compiled with the aid of a committee of scholars the first Arabic-Arabic dictionary. We gave them a considerable amount of support. Among other things, Birge came home during the war and helped us train people in the use of the Arabic language. Lately I heard from his widow, still active in social work in Turkey, that Birge lived to see that dictionary finished and published. It became a working tool for everything in the Arabic world, the first Arabic-Arabic dictionary on common principles— not historical—but common principles, with the definition of each word, the history of its origin and its varied uses, in the same style that we have in the third edition of *Webster's* in English.

4. DIVISION FOR THE HUMANITIES

I. Administration

GARD: You have been saying some very interesting things about programs, developments in foreign nations, and particular projects, but what I was hoping to get at right here, I guess, was the personal problems that you encountered as director of this division, relating perhaps to the assembly of information which might point out directions. I'm trying to look for personal dilemmas that you might have faced. That's pretty hard to answer, perhaps.

STEVENS: Oh, no. We had a weekly conference of officers, where every man judged every other man's program. If we thought his ideas were good, we said so; and we told him so if we thought they weren't so good.

So we got a layout of the next docket in that weekly conference. I had a lot of wonderful men to work with—the other directors, and particularly two presidents, Mason and Fosdick.

In those days, you know, the traditions were pretty strong on what you call "separation of powers." Max was a little bit temperamental, perhaps. He would rarely consult a trustee. He didn't want us to consult a trustee or talk to a trustee before a meeting about our docket items.

GARD: When Max Mason left in 1936, Fosdick came in. What were the major changes when Max left the presidency of the Foundation?

STEVENS: By 1936 Warren Weaver, in Natural Science, was autonomous, let's say. The same was true of Alan Gregg, and for the time being, until he left, the same was true of Edmund Day. I don't think there was too much disturbance. Fosdick was one of those general administrators who knew how to get the most out of you. I would go in and he would say, "Well, what do you have this month, Dave?" When I told him, he would say, "Fine, go ahead!" That's all he ever said, unless part of a program was in a new direction. Once a month he would come to talk separately with his five directors. We were all old enough and had such capable staffs that it didn't so much take supervision as it did protection of what we wanted to do, and to see that we got the money.

GARD: What was your typical day like?

STEVENS: We would write letters from 9:15 to 10:30, see people until noon, have lunch and see some more, write some more letters in the afternoon and go home.

GARD: Was there a lot of travel connected with your work?

STEVENS: I had five officers and at least two of us on the road all the time. When we were out of the office, we had to write up our diaries every night before we went to bed, telling exactly what was said and what promise, if any, and what negative answer we gave. All these diaries turned in by the officers on trips were matched by the diaries we had to write after interviews during the day at the office. We were also to answer all letters within a week of receipt.

There were two other limitations, which no longer exist. In advance of any action we could not make an implied promise, and we were not allowed to take any decorations—I was offered one or two.

GARD: Where did the diary idea originate?

STEVENS: That was an established policy of the Foundation. Another thing you were not allowed to do—odd as it seems now—was to make public speeches or write for publication. One comical result of that was at the time Alan Gregg did make an exception to talk to a big New York dinner — I don't know what it was — but he was introduced by Norman Cousins. Cousins whispered to Alan as they went in, "I've got to go be-

fore your speech. I've got another engagement. But I'll introduce you."
And he did. He introduced him as a man named Gregg from Philadelphia,
told all about him, and Alan let him walk out and never told him of his
gross error, but went on and made his speech.

GARD: In other words, Cousins didn't realize he had the wrong material?
STEVENS: Alan recognized when Cousins started to talk that he wasn't
talking about him. He was talking about a man who lived in Philadelphia,
whose life sketch Cousins' secretary, perhaps, had dug out of *Who's Who*.
So far as I know, Alan told this to no other but me—least of all to Cousins.

We had some odd things about control, over what to do about travel.
We never went out on a call at any institution—in our country, or all the
way to Germany, to Japan, or to South America—until we were two-thirds
convinced we wanted to do it. Frequently an officer returned to location
for a check on need or loss of aim in a term grant, as an item for report
to Board meetings. Also, we had weekly officers' conferences and daily
divisional officers' conferences. We wrote a great many memoranda on
programs. Of course, most of those programs were continuous for a considerable period.

In short, we kept away from public appearance. We kept absolutely
controlled records of what we were doing and saying and promising. All
that, I know, is in the Foundation archives. We also wrote special reports.
I have already mentioned the special board meetings at Christmas time in
Williamsburg, where we presented our new programs and had approval
of what we intended to work at, so as to limit a program down to what
could be managed financially, and to let people know we were not working,
at least for a year, outside fixed areas in each division. At one meeting,
I think I told you, we had a complete review of programs, at which time
Edmund Day reacted so strongly against the criticism of what he was
trying to do that he decided to get out of the Foundation. As I said
earlier, it wasn't long before he became president of Cornell University.

That meeting had its bad effects for many months; officers felt hostile
and some trustees apologetic. The usual relations between officers and
trustees were cordial, as they were among officers. I worked under five
presidents — Arnett, Mason, Fosdick, Chester Barnard, and Dean Rusk.
They were all different, all interesting, and are to be remembered for the
fact that they let us do pretty well what we intended to do.

GARD: You mentioned earlier the anonymity that was required concerning Foundation operations. Could you elaborate on this?
STEVENS: The Foundation didn't carry any operating program except
in Public Health. We gave the money to those who would do what they
said they would. The announcement of the gift was in the hands of the
recipient, until the annual report, when it had to come out. In drama, for

example, we gave our money to the National Theatre Conference and to five or six training centers.

GARD: Was there any reason not to mention the name Rockefeller Foundation?

STEVENS: Well, there is one general reason. You never tell about a grant. You give the beneficiary a chance to use that as a pressure on somebody to get more money. He can tell them what he wants to. It will come out in the annual report, of course. But the Foundation didn't take any credit.

GARD: I think a lot of people are familiar with the idea of a matching grant. I believe John D., III used this idea for obtaining funds for Lincoln Center.

STEVENS: Half of our grants were made with the incentive mode. You get the other people to match it, one dollar for one.

GARD: Did you have occasion specifically to interact with this kind of business?

STEVENS: Oh, yes. We had to negotiate it with them. We would give them a term grant with the understanding that at the end of five years they were on their own. We couldn't be perpetual maintainers of old programs—then we should never have done much.

GARD: What happened before the point you were two-thirds sure of the grant?

STEVENS: You read the documents and got their office calls and built up a pretty clear idea of what was in their proposal. Of course, we knew a lot of these universities and knew the people. We knew what they had in them anyway. And the American Council of Learned Societies was of some help, as they touched all these institutions.

Before long we had fellowship programs running in many areas of humanistic studies, also in drama, and a great many in unusual fields—as in Chinese, Japanese, and Russian—after 1933; and through the war period we had unusual fellowship programs that I can tell you more about. Young operators were coming up for old and entirely new fields of humanistic teaching and research, particularly for war needs abroad, world-wide language and cultural history, and helping bring materials into reach of people in all developed subject fields.

For example, through the ACLS the Foundation was able to bring into action the first abstracting service and the first translating of new Russian material. This was done largely through the vigor of Mortimer Graves. Materials, partly smuggled out through various channels, provided the United States with abstracts and translations, first of medical literature, greatly in demand, and finally of all the fields of knowledge. This was started as an American Council of Learned Societies project.

It grew so rapidly that it soon had a claim on the attention of all scholars and scientists, and then industrialists getting into business in Russia, and soon of all in finance and general trade. The result has been that now the translation and abstraction of Russian materials is a big self-financed program; and it would not have been started without Foundation money. Nobody cared about it in those days, except the people who were aware of the dangers of warfare in the coming years. I don't know what year we started work on that, but the work evolved out of our series of Foundation grants for the making of translations and abstracts of Russian medical papers.

GARD: Was there any direct contact between you and Graves on this project?

STEVENS: Oh, constant. As secretary of the Council, he was really the functioning, creative personality in the group. Graves was a man of ideas, and out-of-the-way ideas, and I would say he was the most active and constant worker in the humanities in the entire period of my work. This is still true today. For example, one of the most recent letters I had from him reported that he was working on a paper for the Council and at the same time making some translations from remote Middle-Eastern languages.

He was the one who broke the furrow, and then we went through with the program of establishing fifty-seven different centers of teaching language in the war pretty much through what Graves and I had talked about and finished. He had as director over him Waldo Leland, a historian, who was cordial and cooperative. I think the strongest ideas came out of Graves and out of his fellowship man, Donald Goodchild; two or three of our best programs in fellowships and in care for displaced scholars were developed more or less from what the ACLS did.

MORTIMER GRAVES: After Dr. David H. Stevens became director for the Humanities of the Rockefeller Foundation, his special interest in the Far East began to be reflected in generous support to ACLS activities in that field of study and those of other institutions in which the ACLS had participant or other concerns. The process began with an interest only in Japan and China, but in time was expanded to include the Slavic world and up to the most supra-national of studies in linguistics. Through the 1930's and 1940's about ninety per cent of the funds to support these enterprises came from the Rockefeller Foundation; without them the later larger programs of the U.S. Government (Army and Navy language programs of World War II and the Federal National Educational Programs in "Language and Area Studies") would have been all but impossible.

II. Officers

STEVENS: Well, the ACLS was then one of our primary tools for big jobs like that, and it was for that reason that I picked a man who worked for them as my first assistant, John Marshall, who had been the secretary of one of their committees and was associated with Harvard. I brought him in as my first man, because he knew how to operate with the ACLS, and from that we moved on so that in the end we had four other assisting directors working in different fields. One was related to our China-Japan program, run by Charles B. Fahs, a man who had Far Eastern backgrounds and was just out of Northwestern University with his doctor's degree in history. We gave him three years of intensive fellowship training in the United States, Paris, and Japan, then brought him in as he left Army duty in Asia and made him responsible for work in the Far East. But long before he was able to operate much, we had done a good deal by use of advisors.

CHARLES B. FAHS: One day in the late winter or early spring of 1933 I received word from my father in New York that I should meet a Dr. Stevens of the General Education Board, who would be in Evanston in a few days. At that time I was working very hard to complete a Ph.D. dissertation on Japan but had no idea how I could continue study of Asia after the degree was earned, or indeed how I could support myself. Of course I kept the appointment. Dr. Stevens was kindly, understanding, noncommittal, as I later discovered Foundation officers have to be. He told me to write him when my dissertation was completed. At the time I did not know how to evaluate the interview. But it led to a G.E.B. fellowship and continued encouragement and support from Dr. Stevens in either his G.E.B. or his R.F. role over many years. Dr. Stevens allowed me, as a fellow, great freedom, though he did not approve my proposals blindly and often helped me to better decisions. I was particularly impressed that he so generously supported my study of Japanese even though I insisted that my field was in the social sciences, not in the humanities, for which he was responsible.

A new relationship began in September, 1946, when, at Dr. Stevens' invitation, I became an assistant director for Humanities in the Rockefeller Foundation. Working under Dave was a great experience. He was genuinely concerned to help the development of the younger men under him. But he taught more by example than by word. Explicitness was never characteristic and even Dave's approvals and disapprovals were often ambiguous. But in fact he encouraged the junior officers to think independently and to make their own contributions to program development. He supported them when they did so.

STEVENS: Then we had a classicist, Edward F. D'Arms, who had taught at the University of Colorado and had been taken into Army duty. He knew Europe. He had been a special service officer in Germany, and he came in and developed a progam first of all related to the Army. He established corps of men to follow the Army in its movement eastward across Germany to salvage and bring out paintings and all kinds of works of art and rare books. His teams, formed by the ACLS, saved materials in museums and libraries, and the works of art were brought to the United States for security. Later on we gave them back to Germany.

D'Arms did admirable service on Foundation programs in Europe until he left about 1957, soon after I retired. He went to the Ford Foundation and helped them develop their total program in the arts and the humanities. He is still working as an advisor with the Ford Foundation as well as for the National Endowment for the Humanities. He was an excellent man who developed our humanities program.

EDWARD F. D'ARMS: Despite my limited foundation experience, Dave never embarrassed me in the meetings which I had arranged and conducted. No one could have been quicker or surer in his grasp of complicated situations than was Dave. He was particularly sensitive to individuals and was prepared to recommend a grant when a person of ability and integrity was involved.

We had long talks on many trips and Dave taught me a great deal about Foundation work in a non-didactic way, through his accounts of earlier Foundation actions. Always the individual, rather than the policy or program, was the determining factor.

STEVENS: We got a man who later went to India. This was Chadbourne Gilpatric. He was a philosophy major at Harvard, and we got him after he had had a period in government. He was useful there. He operated the fellowship program mainly and ended up in carrying out a total program of his own in India. He worked at developing particular branches of the humanities having some relation to philosophy. For example, we organized a project under the help of five outstanding philosophers. Brand Blanshard at Swarthmore was one of them. We picked a team of five philosophers — Max Carl Otto of Wisconsin, Curt J. Ducasse of Brown, Blanshard, Arthur E. Murphy of Illinois, and Charles W. Hendel of Yale as secretary. We financed them for a national tour to visit strategic universities. There would be advance notices sent when they were coming, and the faculties would be invited for three days of conferences. Not only professors from all the outlying schools, universities, and colleges, but businessmen and educational leaders were invited. They covered the entire country. They produced a book which gave the result of their discussions and their recommendations with a digest of their plans for the future. It all had a good deal to do with stimulating general interest in philosophy. Out of it came an East-West philosophical center in Hawaii to which we gave funds, and for three or four years we paid the expense of Chinese, Japanese, and American philosophers to attend summer sessions at the University of Hawaii. Each year they released a book on what they thought were currently important problems and what was being done. The center, still going on at the University of Hawaii, is an effective part of humanistic studies with a defined international scope.

CHARLES W. HENDEL: I returned to the United States in 1940 from McGill University in Montreal. Shortly after arriving, David Stevens got in touch with me, and I found that they needed some honest information about Canadian universities. I had been dean of the Arts and Science faculty at McGill. Naturally, I was hoping that the University there would benefit by any grant from the Foundation, but I didn't slant my report. Stevens quietly took in what I said, and they made their own decision in the light of other information. I was much impressed by his quiet judgment.

I didn't expect to have any dealings whatsoever with the Foundation. For one thing, it was enough to start in with a new Department of Philosophy, but along about 1942 Stevens approached me with a view to my undertaking a survey of the role of philosophy in American education. My answer was that I didn't know enough myself to undertake a survey of that kind, but that I proposed instead to have the American Philosophical Association appoint a special commission. Stevens immediately agreed to my proposal, which I then forwarded to the officers of the Association, and their response was to appoint a commission consisting of five members: Arthur E. Murphy being chairman, Blanshard, C. J. Ducasse, Max C. Otto, and myself as secretary and, so to speak, general manager. We planned, with Stevens at my elbow making suggestions, meetings in Chicago, Berkeley, California; Los Angeles, New Orleans, Baltimore, and New York, and we took testimony from people in each of these places who were meeting in conference with us. The consequence eventually was our publication of a series of studies in "Philosophy in American Education in 1945."

Stevens was very good in suggesting also my participation in Princeton's Humanities Program, the Special Program, as it was called, where

I served as graduate chairman. Stevens also knew all about what was going on in California at that time and let me know the work being done there in the same field. He was a marvelous collaborator, unobtrusively guiding us. You may know, of course, that the program no longer exists at Princeton for the reason that it established the Humanities Division and was no longer needed as a special or pilot program.

STEVENS: I had two other assistant directors, Irving A. Leonard and William Berrien, who opened up a Latin American program. Irving Leonard was a man with a cloistered program in Latin American history. He was one of the few men I thought we could get from the University of California with a background of training under a specialist, one of the great names in South American history, namely Herbert E. Bolton. We got Leonard to go along as an experiment, prospecting in Mexico and elsewhere, and he started in Latin American history. He didn't stay too long, but went to teach.

Then I got another man from the University of California who was a very general and a very capable man who had contacts with people in Latin America. He spoke Portuguese and Spanish so well that he could go into a town, perhaps go to the local tavern, and enjoy conversation with the townspeople for a few minutes or an hour or so and then leave. He talked like a native. The people would say, "Who are you? Did you ever meet me — or what?" Bill Berrien also taught Spanish and Portuguese like a native. He was greatly interested in music and greatly interested in people. I traveled Latin America with him, south of Mexico, twice. Bill was perfect as a negotiator with townspeople.

We had a very good start in Latin America, and we did a good deal of work with individuals and helped men who were historians and linguists, and one or two philosophers. We also met some men who later became active in the Colegio de México. This was the program basically financed by the Mexican government. I talked about it before. It provided quarters and salaries. It wasn't for students so much as it was for scholars and the training in graduate types of work for some younger men. Cosio Villegas, the great creative historian; Zea, a philosopher; and Alfonso Reyes, who was a critic and poet, were surrounded by younger men who finally brought to Mexico City a group of remarkable linguists. As far as I know, they are still very active. The scouting program of Leonard and Berrien covered most of the more highly-cultivated countries. What we are talking about now is the unit that finally bound these countries together in the Colegio de México.

GARD: So there were scholars there from all over Latin America?

STEVENS: That's right.

GARD: What was the relationship between you and your assistant directors?

STEVENS: It was a good one. The division wouldn't have existed if it hadn't been. We had a meeting every morning and laid out the next program of travel and of preparing documents for the executive committee paper work.

GARD: How extensive was your travel?

STEVENS: I traveled about a third of my time. Too much. The last trip was in Germany with D'Arms. I ended up in Ireland on a program I wish we had started long before.

GARD: What was the purpose of most of the trips?

STEVENS: As I said, when you are ready to act on an idea, you are pretty well committed to it mentally before you go out. So if you had a program in language or in history, you sent a man out to see the promising centers where you had new projects and a pretty clear perspective.

GARD: David, what was the process of making a grant in those days of the early years of the Division for the Humanities?

STEVENS: Well, we had all kinds of letters, of course. We had great help from the trustees, because at our Christmas meetings, we had approval of our new plans for the coming year; and we knew how much money we had to spend. We got a great number of requests by mail. We answered them every day by negatives or by temporary holding notices. We didn't leave any mail over night. When I had five officers to help me it was quite simple. Each man had his field of interest, and all the things in his field went to him. It might be that he would pick out some that he would want to talk about in our officers' conference; but about two-thirds of our active business came from our own officers and by recommendations of men all over the country, who we knew were reliable. We would get these materials and discuss them; if we were two-thirds convinced a project was something we wanted to do, we would send a man out to see it, in due course, whether it was South America, or Britain, Europe, or anywhere in the United States. We would get the officer's report back, talk it out pro and con, and probably have some further correspondence. Then we would write up a docket item on an approved item. Eight months of the year (or ten months, perhaps) we had meetings of the Executive Committee, and we would take in these general items, usually saving two or three of the more important ones to represent what we had done, at the annual meeting. Daily we decided for immediate action via fellowships and "grants in aid" for individuals and had action by the president for releases of the funds. As I told you earlier, every one of these items, the names of the people we had talked to, all of this had to go into diaries.

The diaries were mailed back to be typed up and put away in files as an absolute record of what was said and what was promised or not promised. The same kind of records were made and filed for office interviews, too. All contacts were recorded in files for any required proof of status.

GARD: Did you have many problems with people who knew you were a ready source of money and tried to take advantage of that fact?

STEVENS: You never talk about money until you are sure that it's a good idea. So you don't have to bother with the third-class people. They never get below the surface. You talk to a man until you are sure that he has an idea and sure that he will take care of it when you are through helping him. Those are the two tests. The dollars come in last. It isn't like foreign aid.

5. LANGUAGE PROGRAMS

I. Far Eastern Studies for War Duty

STEVENS: Over the years from 1930 to 1950, then, we had a slowly-developing innovative program to build major fields of work. I have talked of a few. I have said nothing of three that are very much to the credit of the Foundation: a program on Far Eastern studies, on American studies, and on drama.

I had a letter the other day about a program of the Foundation in the Far East, asking if I had been interested in the Far East because my wife had lived there for five years as a teacher. That was probably one cause of it. The perfectly obvious reason was that there was so much work to do. Foundation activity on Far Eastern studies began in 1930 and continued until I retired in 1950. One of the fine end products was the first big book on the subject by two Harvard professors, John K. Fairbank and Edwin O. Reischauer. They said, "The Humanities division of the Rockefeller Foundation gave us a head start." They brought out a very unusual basic book on Japan and China, based on their lectures to undergraduates at Harvard, which had been given over a period of years.

JOHN KING FAIRBANK: My recollections of David Stevens are not so much direct as indirect in the early years. As graduate students in Peking in the early 1930's we heard of Mortimer Graves as the executive of ACLS interested in Chinese studies and of David Stevens as the man who backed him and provided funds. The half dozen of us then in Peking had only the vaguest idea as to our futures but these were the two names that seemed to matter in the American scene to which we were returning.

Some years later after becoming settled at Harvard, I had an opportunity to know David Stevens firsthand and appreciate the breadth of his interest and the liveliness of his imagination. He proved to be a warm human being with a natural sympathy for the problems in the pioneer era when an American school of Chinese studies was brought into being.

MORTIMER GRAVES: Early in the 1930's David Stevens asked me to write a memo on the promotion of Chinese and Japanese studies. The point of the memo, as I recall it, was that there was coming up a group of young American scholars for whom there were no college or university posts in sight. Stevens thereupon devised a college package program under which salary on a declining scale over a period of years and contribution to the building up of an appropriate library would be provided to an institution of college or university level which would make a permanent employment in the Chinese or Japanese field. I was to keep my eye out for appropriate institutions. I have heard that some twenty-five appointments were finally made. Some that I recall: George Kennedy at Yale, Robert Reischauer at Princeton, Herrlee Creel at Chicago, Earl Swisher at Colorado, George Taylor at Washington, Charles Burton Fahs at Pomona-Claremont.

STEVENS: Not enough was being done, in 1930, and the government didn't even have it in mind, excepting to develop a few men for duty in the embassies. In 1933 we started giving training fellowships. Between 1933 and 1945 we spent a quarter of a million dollars on language programs, primarily Chinese, Japanese, and Russian. This total program had immediate value for war duty and was also relevant for future foreign communication. We started these operative programs by helping the Navy. The American Council of Learned Societies, with Foundation funds, started a great school at the University of Colorado, for which they recruited a hundred teachers, many of them White Russians who had fled the country. Almost no Americans were available to do any serious work in Japanese for war duties. But we had one woman, daughter of a missionary, Miss Florence Walne, who went in as director of the project and did a superb job. She had a few of our fellows who came to help. The hundred teachers had four hundred students who, for fourteen months talked, read, and thought Japanese—and nothing else. They didn't have any English private conversation. They were supposed to talk in Japanese only.

The Navy was a good taskmaster and got full returns, as did the Army, in essential personnel. These were the men who at the end of their year went out as field workers, some with the Army in the field, where they immediately translated diaries and letters from dead Japanese, or from other sources. Some of them went on into code and cipher and became specialists not only in the language, but in some of the very remote forms of Japanese, which the Japanese Navy used as means of secret communication, thinking that nobody could read them. Our military captured an agent in China with a paper on him that they knew had a secret message. He was a spy all right, but you couldn't condemn a man without first trying to learn what that thing was. One of our advanced fellows, who was attached loosely to Harvard and was in the field in China, was given this document. He read it.

Some of the people working on code got intercepts of messages and solved them. They got a solution of one message which reported details of a Japanese flight that was carrying orders for an attack on the American fleet in the South Seas. This came out of one man's knowledge of the Japanese language and the knowledge of code.

MORTIMER GRAVES: As the 1940's began it became obvious that the United States was about to be involved in world-wide activities which would demand Americans trained in numerous languages, most of which were not presented in American education, and for which there were no American professors or learning materials in English. Early in 1941 the Rockefeller Foundation granted the ACLS what for those days was a very large sum (my recollection is that it was $100,000) for remedying this situation. Since the group of young unemployable American linguistic scientists was already much on my mind and on the minds of my principal linguistic advisors (Franklin Edgerton and Edgar Sturtevant of Yale), it took no great feat of imagination to decide that they were just the people who could contribute to the solution of our problem.

The story of the first appointment made by ACLS from these funds is illustrative though perhaps not typical, for every language later had its own little saga. I was describing the new program to one of my "contacts" in G-2 (Army Intelligence) — a certain Colonel Roberts — and I asked him what languages he would like to see undertaken. This was just at the time the Japanese were on their way to the Indonesian oil fields in construction of the Greater East Asia Co-Prosperity Sphere. Roberts' reply was that at the moment he needed nothing so much as a couple of people who knew Siamese, as we then called Thai.

One of the most readily available "young linguistic scientists" was Dr. Mary R. Haas, who had written grammars and dictionaries on certain Indian languages of the central United States. She was invited to Washington and asked to apply the same kind of linguistic talents to Siamese. At the Siamese Embassy she learned that there was a group of Siamese studying engineering and similar subjects at the University of Michigan. She moved to Ann Arbor and began applying the techniques she had learned through the American Indian languages to describing Siamese. This was the foundation upon which she later produced the textbooks and dictionaries of Thai which are probably even today the best materials available to the American for elementary study of Thai. Other young linguists were similarly put to work on Burmese, Turkish, Chinese, and other languages. This work was proceeding satisfactorily when, suddenly, the Japanese struck at Pearl Harbor.

On that Sunday afternoon, I heard the news of Pearl Harbor on the radio. I went upstairs to my study and wrote a letter to Dr. Haas saying that the time had now come to start teaching as well as tooling. I asked whether she could teach a class in Siamese, using the native speakers to provide the model of speech to be imitated while she presented the scientific linguistic background and controlled the whole presentation. This was the beginning of the so-called "Army method," which got so much advertising after the war.

II. Chinese, Japanese, and Russian Studies

STEVENS: Besides the Japanese branch, at Boulder, Colorado, we had equally fine Chinese programs. We had a marvelous man at Yale named George Kennedy; another man, an Englishman named George Taylor, who started a new school in Russian at Berkeley and next as head of a big Far Eastern school at the University of Washington; and particularly at Columbia, where three unusual men — Goodrich, Robinson, and Henderson — created not only the school of work in language and literature, but opened the present fine program of studies in Chinese and Japanese for all fields. L. Carrington Goodrich had much to do for our national program at Columbia on all aspects of Far Eastern studies and Russian studies as advisor, as did Owen Lattimore. The one that we didn't help much was the unusual school at Harvard, the famous Harvard-Yenching Institute, which had a large endowment. Its director, a Frenchman named Serge Elisséeff, was a great organizer and a practical scholar, with long experience and in touch with specialists elsewhere. His guidance helped George Fairbank, Edwin Reischauer, Robert Reischauer, and others.

On Russian studies, I told of the translation project initiated by Mortimer Graves. One of the men in Chinese studies I ought to mention again before I drop that. George Kennedy had lived as a boy in Shanghai and had made friends with the younger generation of Chinese. He came on through his training in American university backgrounds and became a leader in the operation of an important center for Chinese studies in Yale

University. He and other men also produced the important basic text-books, small study books, and dictionaries for student use throughout the country. He was a tiger for work and he picked his own students. He chose people who were strong in general studies and had good language sense, with interest in Chinese. He did it in a way that never failed. He made them use Chinese characters and learn them faithfully. He had a big font of Chinese characters and had his students set type and print in order to realize the meaning of symbols by using them.

Oddly enough, the irony of George's story is that we arranged to send him back to China after the war in order to work with Chinese scholars, and our government wouldn't let him go. Why? Because as a young man, living in Shanghai, he had a great many friends. He then had an article, in his early days, in a magazine that had the label of communist, and probably was. He wrote that one article when a young man, and as a result our government wouldn't let him go out thirty years later. It was similar to the treatment that McCarthy gave Owen Lattimore for his work in Outer Mongolia and Tibet. McCarthy's accusation was based entirely on a photograph showing Lattimore with a group of avowed communists. But he was there learning, not cooperating. McCarthy made a whipping boy of Owen Lattimore and nearly ruined him; but Owen kept on going and is still working.

Our fellows in Far Eastern and Slavic studies are bringing up the next generation. In short, I think the Foundation can take the credit for building Far Eastern studies into the American system.

GARD: How did the Reischauers fit into this scheme?

STEVENS: Robert and Edwin Reischauer were among the finest young American scholars to work in Japanese studies. They were the children of missionaries, spent their boyhood in Japan, took degrees in the United States, and became identified with the Harvard-Yenching Institute.

GARD: Did you give them any support?

STEVENS: We may have in the case of Robert. Robert Reischauer became the first man to write a history of the Japanese royal tradition, destroying the fallacy of divine origin. He was on the faculty at Princeton then. When he finished the book, knowing that he would never be admitted to Japan after its publication under conditions that then existed, he got up a study group and took it to Japan, and from there went on to Shanghai. He was in a hotel in Shanghai when the Japanese made an attack, and he was killed in that attack. But his brother, Edwin, our ambassador to Japan for five years, is now back at the Harvard-Yenching Institute and the all-university Far Eastern Center. He is one whose influence ought to have been far greater with the politicians than it has been.

EDWIN O. REISCHAUER: I looked upon David Stevens as a sort of patron saint of what we now call East Asian studies. His interest in developing the field in the 1930's and the support he gave to a few well-selected individuals were in large part responsible for the fact that the United States did have at least a handful of well-trained scholars by the beginning of World War II who could help shape our successful response to the crisis in language training and intelligence work. These scholars then trained, at government expense, a large wartime corps of experts, who then became the backbone of the field and account for its phenomenal development in the thirty years since the war.

Burton Fahs and George Kennedy are good examples. My brother Robert would have been one also but for his untimely death. I know that part of his training was supported by the Rockefeller Foundation, though the rest was financed by the Harvard-Yenching Institute. He was at graduate school at Harvard from 1931 to 1933, then in Japan from 1933 to 1934, and then at the Library of Congress doing research work before he got his position at Princeton in 1935 or 1936. He was leading a study tour from Princeton when he was killed in August, 1937, by Chinese bombs aimed at a Japanese warship in the river at Shanghai.

I myself actually never received Rockefeller support, being carried throughout my training by the Harvard-Yenching Institute, but David Stevens' interest and moral support certainly encouraged me in my studies and backed up my morale. To me he seemed a very kindly patron saint. I attributed this in part to the fact that his wife before marriage had taught in Japan and become a close friend of my parents, but I have no doubt that he was as kindly to others without such personal contacts. I remember what a boost to my morale I received in the summer of 1933 when he had me appointed as one of the American delegates to a scholarly international conference on linguistics, I believe it was. I was only 22 and just finishing my second year of graduate study, and of course nothing like this had ever happened to me before. My self-confidence was much bucked up by this, though in fact I was unable to attend, since my plans called for me to go to France for two years at that point.

By the time I returned from studying abroad in 1938 the field had become much more developed. For several years after that it seemed to me that the chief force encouraging its growth was the activity of the American Council of Learned Societies under Mortimer Graves, but behind Mortimer stood the financial support and interest of David Stevens and the Rockefeller Foundation, which thus continued to be the prime moving force.

STEVENS: On these Far Eastern language programs, which were the slowest to mature, starting in 1933, we spent as much as six years on a few men and sent them to Europe or the Far East. That's where we got some of our major figures today. We started early in the General Education Board, getting ready for our work in the Far East and in Russia.

I didn't tell you the beginning of our aid to Slavic studies was in only one man who had any scholarly standing. He was George Patrick at Berkeley. He was the only American professor who in 1930 had much knowledge of Russia, of its literature, history, and language, and of oral Russian. Another man, Sam Harper at the University of Chicago, had a social interest in Russia. Mortimer Graves, who motivated these three programs, was back of Ernest Simmons, who for years at Columbia University trained a great many men. Because Simmons had been in Russia and was well accepted by communist scholars before the war, Graves engineered an invitation for Simmons to try to break the ice after World War II and get us back in contact with all Russian scholars. Graves arranged in Washington to have Simmons admitted to Russia, and we sent him over. He came back completely frustrated. His old friends wouldn't meet or even come to see him, except at night. They didn't dare to be seen talking to him; and except for a few formalities, his trip was a failure. But that didn't stop Simmons; he spent the rest of his life, of course, training Americans.

Another field of activity was Great Britain, where we gave aid to scholars in Russian, Chinese, and Japanese. One of our fellows, Homer Dubs, trained on Foundation fellowships, went to Oxford to teach Chinese. I think he's still there. We supported one of the outstanding teachers of Russian, a British writer named Richard Hare, working at the University of London. Here at home we prepared fellows, paid their salaries for two or three years, and provided their libraries. Herrlee Creel, head of Chinese research at the University of Chicago, had a "head start" by long residence in China. He went there as a young man, with no money, and lived as a native. He is now a world authority on early Chinese history and culture. His first book, which will never be outmoded, is *The Birth of China*. Then two who should be listed are Knight Bickerstaff at Cornell University and Arthur Hummel, then at the Library of Congress, and finally a strange man named Karl A. Wittfogel, a German, who had lived long years in China and knew the substance of their chronicle histories. When he came over, we took a chance on him. Although he had the label of being communist, and so was badgered and kicked around, he finally was taken in and settled at Columbia. He became an outstanding scholar, interpreting Chinese history, and he was taken to the University of Washington by George Taylor to help set up his school.

GEORGE TAYLOR: In 1941 David Stevens called me in, apparently on someone's recommendation, as I did not know him, to ask for my opinion of the work being done by Dr. K. A. Wittfogel under a Rockefeller Foundation grant. He asked only one main question: Is the man a serious scholar and does he know what he is doing? After a few months of investigation I reported back to David that Wittfogel was serious and was engaged in an original approach to the interpretation of Chinese society. David decided to continue supporting the Wittfogel project, which produced, among other things, a volume on *Liao*, published by the American Philosophical Society, and *Oriental Despotism*, published by Yale University Press. At the close of World War II David Stevens offered me a grant to use in the promotion of foreign area studies and this was accepted by the University of Washington. I think of David Stevens as a man who was willing to use risk capital to give new ideas a chance.

HERRLEE CREEL: I first came to Dr. Stevens' attention while he was assistant to the president of the University of Chicago and I was a graduate student. I had become determined to study China, even though the University had no program in that field, and I wrote my dissertation on Chinese philosophy in the Department of Comparative Religion. It was published as a book—unfortunately, since it was a very bad book because I knew nothing—but this probably helped to cause me to be awarded a fellowship by the American Council of Learned Societies for 1930-31.

I was to study at Harvard, and by good fortune there was there at that time a rather eminent Chinese scholar, Mei Kuang-ti, who took me on rather literally as a disciple in the Confucian sense. He tutored me for two hours a day for two years. This cramming nearly killed me, but did give me the rudiments of a Chinese classical education. I was given a fellowship for 1931-32 by Harvard-Yenching Institute, and again for 1932-33 by the ACLS.

The funds for my ACLS fellowships had come from the Rockefeller Foundation, and when my Harvard-Yenching fellowships came to an end in the summer of 1935 Mr. Stevens gave me a Rockefeller Foundation fellowship to carry me on to the end of that year, when I came to the University of Chicago.

In my first year on the faculty of the University of Chicago my salary was paid by a fellowship from the Rockefeller Foundation. The Foundation, and Mr. Stevens in particular, played a cardinal role in launching the Far Eastern program in this university. Mr. Stevens encouraged and even urged me to develop a new method for teaching literary Chinese. Foundation funds made it possible to have a staff for this purpose and to publish three volumes of *Literary Chinese by the Inductive Method,* which I am told has played a role in the education of a number of scholars in this and other countries. The Foundation also provided funds that made it possible to lay the foundations—something in the neighborhood of 100,-000 volumes I would guess—of the University's Far Eastern Library. I have been told that this collection (by now, of course, a great deal larger) is estimated to include the most important collection of books on the Chinese classics outside of the Far East. Because those books were acquired before the Second World War they were not only bought relatively cheap, but included items that it might not be possible to purchase today.

GARD: Was there much work in the humanities in Africa?

STEVENS: If you are talking about starting off and going into the jungle, the British were well ahead of us. Well ahead of us, and one very exciting example I can give you is of the year the German, the French, and the British came to us with proposals of what they wanted to do in Africa. There was a British-German-American committee, trying to coordinate all the work there in missionary work and agriculture. As they started they discovered they didn't know how to do it, because they couldn't approach the people. The British had the smartest answer—start in learning the language and put it into print. They had to get informants. Ida Ward, of the University of London, was the leader of their work in England. She proved the impossible to be possible by creating written from oral language. She used informants, some of them students in Great Britain, bringing others, to talk about things so others could take down their oral language, start to codify it, and then to create a grammar, and then get a vocabulary, and then start training teachers. When Ida Ward got through working with Ibo, in ten years they had a book written by an African native that sold 10,000 copies. This proves just what you can germinate by starting at the right spot.

GARD: Did the Rockefeller Foundation contribute to Ida Ward's program?

STEVENS: We gave some money, but it was helped strongly by the London School of African Studies, which the British were far-sighted enough to create and develop. There were two people, Ida Ward and a linguist named Lloyd James, who were at the heart of that little program.

Of course, it takes years. That's what has been going on ever since, at a few of these wartime centers. The best example I happen to know is at Indiana University, where we had a great gathering of specialists in out-of-the-way languages, especially Near Eastern ones. Indiana in the

1930's and 1940's had a very liberal president, Herman B. Wells. As a result, some of the best language work on unusual languages is now lodged at Indiana University, with men trained by the Foundation.

These were supplemented during the war by natives, whom we brought over in large numbers from these African and Asian areas to speak their languages for oral transcripts and analysis, in order to build grammars out of oral speech. We called them informers, but they were really informants. They came and were recorded under the direction of skilled teachers and linguists. They built up textbooks and followed that with the training of men from here and from other countries to teach, write, and so to affect all future events in undeveloped areas. They are creating the substance for knowing languages of the world.

6. AMERICAN STUDIES

I. American Literature and American Studies

GARD: David, you mentioned earlier that the development of American studies was one of your primary concerns when you took the job with the Foundation. You had it on your mind. What did you hope to accomplish?

STEVENS: I think I told you earlier that I had three or four convictions when I took this job. The most important was that the humanities would never live unless they lived in people. Our first job was to help the individual succeed promptly, whereas he would succeed only in a limited way without help. I'm sure I mentioned people who had been on my mind in the field of American literature. One of them I know I mentioned was Curtis Hidden Page, who brought out a large collection of American writings, poetry particularly, which was the basis of some courses in colleges. He had taught at Dartmouth and was at Northwestern. At our own university, the University of Chicago, we had a popular undergraduate lecturer, Percy Boynton.

The editor and teacher noted may well have typified the narrow range of concern in college and university at the undergraduate level before 1930. The contrast with care and time given the British literary tradition was striking. It required a lowering in barriers for research within graduate schools so that themes were accepted for periods and topics beyond mid-seventeenth century limits; then American subject matter had some chance of approval for thesis subjects in graduate schools.

Meanwhile and long before 1930, isolated scholars within Eastern universities were forecasting through their methods of analysis and of critical writing what would be the potential of their students in time to come.

For example, Columbia University had its pioneer in George Edward

Woodberry, whose studies in Emerson were notably ahead of others from his time. His great support to advance of scholarly treatment came in 1907, when he laid down rules on method and substance widely influential in his own years of teaching and far beyond. In 1903-04 the ten-volume edition of the prose and poetry had its beginning. Biographical treatments had begun with that of Edward Waldo Emerson in 1889, to be continued by his son. These were signs on the road to the Columbia tradition of eminence in study of Emerson centered in the name of Ralph L. Rusk.

The writings of Walt Whitman had popular and intensive attention long before 1930. The "complete" works out in 1902 and the later authoritative edition of *Leaves of Grass* heightened scholarly interest; this appears clearly from the bibliographies on Whitman in *The Cambridge History of American Literature* (1917-21). Again, as was true of the 1906 Life of Emerson by Bliss Perry, the Henry Seidel Canby *Walt Whitman* had advantages from scholarly studies.

In Shakespearian scholarship, the American tradition was far behind the British, in time and in variety. But in 1871 Howard Furness set up a landmark with the first of his Variorum series on the plays, carried on by the son of this graduate of Harvard. Studies in every aspect of the life and works of Shakespeare became common after 1930; they were numerous before. Early quality is seen in the John Quincy Adams *Life* (1923) based on that research.

American ways in literary research appear similarly in work with Milton. Once more far behind the British, the American approach was to be unusual in the trend set by J. Holly Hanford. His mastery of the wide body of source materials and control of essential language gave momentum to his school of study. His work and my own had full expression before 1930, far ahead of the fine and fundamental work done by Douglas Bush and his contemporaries. Milton, Shakespeare, Whitman, and Emerson are examples of those well examined by American scholars before the break toward American studies after 1930.

Then, as the rigid limitations within British materials before the mid-seventeenth century broke down, the turn to later periods brought American literature into full acceptance; acceptable theses for the master's and doctorate degrees yielded a source of materials for hundreds of candidates to work in our untilled fields.

Surely there were others; then there was this special school at Vanderbilt, which was breaking ice and starting new things in criticism. But I can't remember in the large universities, before 1930, any large concern for American literature or language. There wasn't anything in the way of literary criticism in the curriculum of graduate studies as there is now.

We had plenty of good American political historians but very few social historians.

I should give Ronald S. Crane at Chicago more credit than I do, for turning off into a new direction of literary analysis. He resisted, on a mild basis, the style in which I. A. Richards analyzed and taught literature. One of the worst confrontations I ever witnessed was when we brought Richards from Cambridge to Harvard, and paid his salary for five years. I introduced him to a few literary and critical scholars of America by having a big meeting in Washington at which Crane and his philosopher friend, Richard McKeon, were present. They just ragged Richards vigorously, and I didn't think too much of that.

Richards was a great dynamo. He talked like an angel, and he had ideas. He said that the basis of literary study is, first of all, the use of metaphor. You have to see what the symbolism is and see where it leads you. An example of this method is what the Harvard professor of English, John Livingston Lowes, did in his work. He traced Coleridge's reading to discover the sources of his poetry.

GARD: How did all of this begin to take shape?

STEVENS: In American studies, besides the two men I mentioned, we financed the *Linguistic Atlas of New England*. This was the first of many, covering large areas, to define origins of the people by the forms of their language and local dialects. These studies created a solid basis for social studies, widening old forms of historical interpretation.

For all future developments in interpretations of American literature we financed a definitive study brought to us by Professor Robert E. Spiller of the University of Pennsylvania. He was to produce, with the help of collaborators, a new literary history of the United States. This would be a single project, well planned, of which he would be the editor, with some fifty other scholars who would in their free time work intensively on assigned parts of a complete plan. Most of them did not have scholarships or fellowships. They were men doing full-time university teaching.

I can remember talking with Spiller on the day when he outlined this, and he said, "If you give me fifteen thousand dollars, we'll put this thing through and bring it to a publisher and get it out. A good part of this money will go to Thomas H. Johnson, at Lawrenceville School, who is to do all the bibliographies." We gave them the money, and they brought out the first scholarly history, in three volumes, a beautiful job, that put our own literary history at once on a high level for popular appreciation of its value.

ROBERT E. SPILLER: I was chairman of a committee which was initiated by the American Literature Group of the Modern Language Association to undertake the project which was later to become the *Literary History of the United States,* with the promise of publication by the Macmillan Company of New York.

In 1940, the Group voted to postpone the project indefinitely, and Henry Seidel Canby and I drew together a private group of editors. Willard Thorp of Princeton was asked to join the group as an editor, and Thomas H. Johnson as bibliographer. Stanley T. Williams of Yale, Howard Mumford Jones of Harvard, and Dixon Wecter of California were invited to be associates. The project was reduced in scale to two volumes of historical text and one of bibliography.

The ACLS made a grant of $1,000 to finance meetings of editors and contributors, and the Macmillan Company advanced $10,000 against royalties. The editors set up a budget of $30,000, not counting their own expenses, and expected to publish with a deficit. Meanwhile, they began a search for possible subsidy.

Discussions were opened with David H. Stevens and John Marshall of the Rockefeller Foundation early in 1943. A direct grant to a private group was out of line with Foundation policy, but fellowship grants for specific work to individuals seemed possible. Two such grants of $5,000 were made in September of 1943 to Swarthmore College for my work and to Princeton University for Willard Thorp. Two years later a similar grant of $5,000 was made to the Lawrenceville School for Thomas H. Johnson, making a total of $15,000. Without this aid the work, now in its fourth edition and generally accepted as the authority in its field, might not have been possible.

STEVENS: In history, literature, and language we opened up new areas. Take Tom Clark, at the University of Kentucky. He had a wonderful idea, to find the trails of all the pioneer settlers of the southern states. He developed an entire program for every state by itself, and also interlaced the parts, showing who went, where they went, and in this way got the basis of early pioneer life in the South. We paid for field work, study, and eventual printing of the eight volumes of books—of course, one was Clark's own—on the growth of American life through the traders and the traveling teachers and scholars. Aid for these directives through scholarship opened up the primitive South intellectually. This series could never have been done without philanthropy.

In criticism, we had some who were in teaching, as was one of the Fugitive writers, John Crowe Ransom. He started a journal, the *Kenyon Review,* which had a great deal of influence on writing of contemporary criticism. He also was a poet. His great influence was among younger men, toward how to teach, what to teach, and how to approach critical writing. Then in New York, we had a professional or two, like Alfred Kazin, a brilliant critic, still writing. We helped him with two or three of his books.

Then we had other teachers appearing in American studies. There was John Dodds at Stanford, brother of a president of Princeton, and Henry Nash Smith, whom we trained on a fellowship and gave grants toward writing his first book, *Virgin Land*. He became one of the leading teachers and research men at Berkeley. The list of our fellows is long, their names listed in the Rockefeller Foundation reports to 1970.

GARD: How did the Foundation get involved with the group of writers and critics known as the "Fugitives," and specifically with Ransom?

STEVENS: We knew about him. We read the literature, saw the documents, and went to see him. We got him started on more help for his own journal and for training other men.

GARD: Were you working against any kind of ambivalent attitude toward the Fugitives on the part of other scholars?

STEVENS: I'm sure we were.

GARD: And that didn't bother you.

STEVENS: I don't know of anything that bothered us, no. I gave you a good example in the reception given Ivor A. Richards. There is no question where my sympathy was there. It was with the man who was creating—not criticizing.

GARD: What about the people you saw who were not given funding?

STEVENS: You see a lot of wonderful people, idealists. Almost two-thirds of the people you see are exciting people to talk to, and you make one of two or three kinds of decision. You think, maybe he could do it, or his university ought to help him, or we don't have money in that area to do it. So up to the limit of our money, we tried to pick the best of them, of course. There was a fellow out at Stanford by the name of Dixon Wecter. He was not getting any help, to speak of. He got his chance finally to be the official editor of the Mark Twain papers. That put him on a level where he had a right to make claims. He got going beautifully, and we gave him some help. He also did some good field work for us. He was a very unusual man in his group. He didn't belong to any school; he went out on his own. He was a pioneer, doing research on Mark Twain.

Dumas Malone is another good example. He came down from Columbia University for help to get him going on his life of Jefferson. When he came to see me, he said, "I'm on the fence here at Columbia; I've got to teach or I've got to research this subject. If you give me ten thousand dollars this year and maybe for another year, you'll never hear from me again." He went ahead and turned out his volumes on the life of Jefferson, and he kept at it. He has just now finished the last one, in retirement.

GARD: When a man comes to you like that, who has an idea for a critical study, does he present to you what he is going to do and why he is going to do it?

STEVENS: Oh, sure. Take Spiller's three-volume history of American literature. That was his own idea. But he said, "I'm not going to try to do it. I can't do it. I need more men. And all we need is enough money to have the free time to get away to research." We got off cheap in that bargain. He could have used a hundred thousand dollars, and we gave him only fifteen. These fellows were devoted, they were determined; you could see that they would do it.

GARD: Would it be fair to say that your initiative, your ability to begin work in this direction, resulted in the creation of American studies?

STEVENS: Well, I wouldn't say that. But I would say I had a part in it.

GARD: Without the Rockefeller Foundation, Division for the Humanities, how long would it have taken to make American studies an essential part of the study of the humanities in this country?

STEVENS: I don't know. You know, the dam had to break some time. There were more plausible thesis subjects back there in our field when they opened up the seventeenth and eighteenth centuries; and the same in American — my God, they have gone wild over it. Now everyone is running into American studies. You don't have to know any Latin or Greek, and you can get away with it—and do a good job at that. And there is a great deal to do that has never been touched.

TOM CLARK: In 1947 I made application to the Rockefeller Foundation for a grant to be used in subsidizing eight or ten scholars in the preparation of as many volumes on travels in the South. I had in mind doing for the South what Reuben Gold Thwaites had done for the early West. I had a reply from David Stevens saying that the Foundation was favorably enough impressed with the request to follow it up to the point of making a direct personal investigation. Mr. Stevens said the Foundation liked to see the applicant and to visit his study and office to form some surface impression of his working habits and conditions.

When Mr. Stevens came to Lexington, I showed him my office, my study, and took him through the University of Kentucky Library. I had just finished work on both the *Southern Country Store* and the *Southern Country Newspaper*. The records from which *Pills, Petticoats, and Plows* was written, and they were indeed voluminous, were lying on the basement floor of the library. He asked me why I did not make a request for a grant to have those arranged and calendared. I did and the Foundation gave us a $10,000 grant in addition to the amount I requested for the travel study.

I met with the prospective editors and the publisher in Atlanta in April, 1947. After long discussion it was decided that no one knew enough about travel literature to select ten volumes for editing. What was needed was a thorough and critical bibliography of the travel books pertaining to the South. Thus it was that we changed course slightly. The result was that between 1947 and 1962 we produced *Travels in the Old South*, *Travels in the Confederacy*, and *Travels in the New South*. Though the six volumes comprised a full unitary study, the volumes were published in three series.

This project turned out to be a much more complex one than I had anticipated in the beginning. An intensive hunt was necessary to make as complete a bibliography as possible, and it was also necessary for me to acquaint myself with the contents of the travel accounts in order to do an intelligent job of editing. Fortunately we had trained bibliographical help which assisted us materially in placing entries in the proper format.

Though I have been an active scholar for almost a half century, nothing I have done, or expect to do, will be more important than this bibliography, which received first-rate reviews; but more important, it has been accepted as a standard work in both the southern and national areas of travel literature. Actually the travelers included figured as prominently in the national scene as in the regional one.

ALFRED KAZIN: I had a Rockefeller grant to work in the Huntington Library on Blake in 1944, and I went to Britain early in 1945 to study the popular education movements in the Army and trade unions there. The one thing I can say about Mr. Stevens at this date is that I owe him a very great deal for his interest in my work. I remember with the deepest gratitude his major role in getting me to England and his sympathetic reading of the manuscripts I submitted on my work, *The Education of Soldiers*. He is a man of spare speech who said exactly what he meant and never overdid anything. My work in England was of the greatest importance in my own development, and it gave me just the chance I wanted to see Britain in what was still its finest hour.

HENRY NASH SMITH: I should warn you at the outset that I have reached the point described by Mark Twain when he said that he used to remember everything, but when he got old he could remember only the things that did not happen.

My memory, then, is that I first met David Stevens in the early 1940's, during the Second World War, at a time when I was a member of the Department of English at the University of Texas in Austin. As the end of the war drew near I applied for a fellowship at the Huntington Library (for the academic year 1945-46) and was granted one, but the stipend was so small I could not support my family on it and would have been unable to accept it had not the Rockefeller Foundation granted me a generous supplementary fellowship. At some point during the academic year 1944-45, I believe I met David Stevens, probably through Dixon Wecter of the Huntington Library staff; but whether I met Stevens in Austin or somewhere else I am not sure. I seem to remember his being in my house in Austin at one point for an evening's talk, but my wife can not recall such an evening, and her memory is better (or should I say less inventive?) than mine. I am fairly certain that Stevens came through San Marino at some point during the year we finally spent there (1946-47).

I should explain that in the summer of 1945, just after VE day, as I was preparing to set out for the Huntington Library, the English Department at Harvard invited me as a visiting lecturer in American literature, and I wanted to take advantage of this opportunity to gain important teaching experience. Stevens amiably postponed my Rockefeller grant for a year, as did Dixon Wecter, and my family and I spent the academic year 1945-46 in Cambridge. It seems logical that Stevens should have come through Cambridge during that winter but I am, again, not certain. Certainly I had a couple of long conversations with him during the two-year period 1945-47, and we exchanged one or two letters about my work and plans. I regarded him as a generous, wise, and of course infinitely knowledgeable academic adviser. I should have liked to have had the opportunity of knowing him much better; I think we could have become real friends. But we never had that opportunity.

DUMAS MALONE: The importance of the support of the Rockefeller Foundation in the early stages of my work on my comprehensive biography of Thomas Jefferson can hardly be exaggerated, and the part that David Stevens played in this was crucial.

I had been engaged on this project for some months when the Foundation made me a three-year grant ($6000 each year plus $1000 each year for expenses). As I recall, I ran into David Stevens at a meeting somewhere, and he asked me if they could do anything to help. Grants were made to institutions rather than to individuals, and at the moment I was without official academic connection, though I was working at the University of Virginia. President Newcomb appointed me honorary consultant in biography to the library there. The grant was made to that university and was administered by it even after I went to Columbia.

Before David Stevens talked with me about my undertaking, it had probably been mentioned to him by Douglas S. Freeman, then a member of the Rockefeller board. At the time I was engaged on the phase of Jefferson's life that was afterwards dealt with in my first volume, and under other circumstances I might never have gone beyond that despite my prognostications to my publishers. At Freeman's suggestion, I described a project covering Jefferson's entire life (which I then thought I could encompass in four volumes) and thus I further committed myself to the larger work.

But for the Rockefeller grant, I might never have finished the first volume and begun the second. After the publication of my second volume the project was virtually suspended for some years. I shall always be grateful to the Rockefeller Foundation for helping me get it started, and I shall never forget the sympathetic understanding of it by David Stevens.

II. A Reminiscence of J. Frank Dobie

GARD: Dave, you once told me an interesting anecdote about Frank Dobie of Texas, who was one of the great regional historians in the country. I wonder if you can remember what happened when he called you that night when you were in Montclair.

STEVENS: The episode that you refer to started in New York City. Frank Dobie, one of the great Texas historians and writers, had been selected to go to Cambridge to lecture on American life and education. He was a maverick, of course—that was his great characteristic. He had been in New York on the way to Cambridge. In the early days of flying, it wasn't sure what day you would go. He had been there nearly a week; during that week I had been entertaining him and having a great time.

One morning during his week in New York City, as I came into my office, Frank was there waiting. The first question was, "Did you ever see the horn museum, David?"

"No, I've never seen the horn museum. What is it?"

Well, he told me that up at the zoo in New York City is a famous hall, where all the big game hunters, such as Teddy Roosevelt, brought back the horns they got from their animal kills. We walked out to get there by way of the subway, and passed a second-hand store. Frank, sucking his long-shanked pipe, said, "I wonder if they've got any horns in here?" Well, we went in, and the big Norwegian owner and his big Labrador dog met us at the front door. He and Frank started to talk. We stayed there an hour, and at the end of the hour they were down on the floor drawing a little design in the dust to show something they wanted to explain to each other. So we left, and outside Frank looked up at the building and said, "Well, we didn't find any horns, but we had a good time." That was the way we spent the week.

I was home, then, along say on the sixth day, and got a telephone call. It was Frank, and I said, "What are you doing here? I thought you had gone." "No," he said, "they put us off another night. So I'm stuck here until two-thirty in the morning, when we are supposed to start. Why don't you come in and have a visit?" This was along about nine o'clock in the evening. I said, "Well, I'm sitting in my shirt sleeves, reading a book." He said, "Come on in; we'll talk." So I got on a bus and went to the Roosevelt Hotel. We lay around and talked until two o'clock, and then went over to the place where the passengers were to be picked up by the bus to go to the airport. This was on the second floor at the top of a moving stairway. As we stood up at the top of the stairway, up came a head above the edge of the floor, and Frank said, "Good morning, how are you?" It turned out to be the wife of Mr. Knopf, the publisher. She was going over, too, and she had with her a handful of beautiful flowers. Frank, in his usual drawl, said, "Are those the same flowers you brought yesterday?" She said no. Then he turned to me and said, "You know, David. I haven't got any American money. What have you got? Any?" And I said, "Yes, I have three dollars and a half; but it takes me a half dollar to get home on the bus. I'll give you three dollars." "Well," he said, "I'll give you a check for it." He wrote me out a check which I didn't look at, but put in my pocket. The next morning I found it was a treasure I ought to have kept and sold for a hundred dollars, because Frank had made the check out to "Three dollars," for "Three dollars," and signed his name; and in my silliness I sent it back to his wife in Austin, Texas, and got a legitimate three dollars back. That check would have been a prize for a collector of autographs!

Frank's total year in Cambridge is put away in a book called *A Texan in England*—a marvelous book. It tells of his experiences in his hall, with the faculty and with the students, living the life of an English teacher, whereas he was a complete outlander from the United States. This book has some remarkable passages about such historic spots as the great American cemetery at Cambridge with its rows and rows of headstones for men brought back from the Continent, killed in the Second World War. Frank's reception was just what you would expect it to be. He was beloved by everybody, and he gave them an insight into the United States. He had, perhaps, more or less learned what he knew about the formal history and culture of the United States after studying for this job. Frank was a writer and a traveler through his own state and wrote wonderful books about the Southwest. This was his first adventure into higher education abroad.

GARD: How did you get associated with Frank Dobie in the first place?

STEVENS: Well, we were working on this American program, especially on regional projects, as at the University of Oklahoma and the University of Texas, helping the men who were striving to get books written and to get them printed. An example is Savoie Lottinville's University Press at Norman, Oklahoma, with its magnificent series of books on the life of the American Indian and on early pioneers. Frank, in the same way, in Texas had been gathering folk tales, scores and scores of stories that never would have been preserved except by this boy who had grown up on a Texas ranch, had ridden horses since he was a little boy, and knew Mexico along the border, as well as all about Southern Texas. I went to see Frank, of course, on a project; and we gave a good deal of money to him and others in Texas for their regional writing.

There was one very fine, fiery fellow named J. Evetts Haley, who had grown up in the panhandle, and was a rancher by birth and nature — a true Texan in loyalties. He was brought in to the University of Texas as a social science research worker and writer. We helped him some on gathering materials. One of his big projects was driving through the country with a truck and going to all the towns and county seats and gathering papers. He brought truckloads of Texas history and stored them in the library. This was in the period when Franklin D. Roosevelt was trying to do what we are trying to do today—rescue the country from a depression—but a little differently, in that it wasn't our kind of depression, but due to an overplus of food. So Roosevelt had set up a program of slaughtering cows and paying the farmers for their losses.

Haley didn't, as a cattleman, endure this thing of Franklin Roosevelt's; so he wrote a piece for the *Saturday Evening Post* called "Cow Business or Monkey Business?" As soon as that was published and traveled over the country, he was fired. His museum, at the University in Austin, was turned over to a novice, who didn't know anything about it and changed labels on his exhibits. One thing that I remember was that Haley had found a fine saddle from an old cattle rancher and had put it up on a pedestal with the name of the man and where it came from. When he went in to show me the museum, his label had been taken down, and on it was written, "Old saddle of a cowboy." He said, "That's typical of their ignorance and their stupidity."

Well, Frank and I had great talks across the table under the trees and at the little brook which ran through his place in Austin, hearing the mockingbirds, and talking about plans and people to help. On one occasion I was in Austin at the home of Henry Nash Smith, with a group of people on the day this book, *A Texan in England,* came out. I bought the first copy at the bookstore and carried it to this little social gathering. Frank wrote in it a marvelous tribute to my wife, saying he wished she were there. We were listening to the broadcast of the first meetings of the United Nations, in San Francisco, when discourses on the future of the world were at a new level of activity.

GARD: Could you describe the first time you met Frank?

STEVENS: He was taking me from Austin up to Lampasas, where he said there was a good stone hotel, where I could get a bus to Oklahoma City. I was going to Oklahoma City on a job. We had a lot of interests there. We must have driven—I don't know how many miles—we took all day, perhaps. We stopped at the grave of Sam Bass, the great desperado, which was nothing but a little dusty spot of chips, because all the fool curiosity seekers who came there had chipped off pieces of his stone. We went on to this town of Lampasas, with Frank telling me Texas stories all the way across, through fields of bluebonnets, the state flower of Texas. There were great meadows of them, and we crossed little bridges, seeing these little streams, with the borders lined with live oaks. We got to Lampasas and had a real Texas country dinner, and Frank put me on the bus for Oklahoma City. That was my first visit with Frank, and it began a friendship that didn't end.

7. PROGRAMS IN DRAMA

I. College and Community Drama

GARD: You have said quite a bit about the background of basic Foundation work in the humanities. I wonder if we could take it on the other side of the Foundation base and say a word about the groundwork in the arts.

STEVENS: Well, one of the two things seen as important was to do something related to the broad public interest of certain colleges and communities, and perhaps the nation as a whole, in the performing arts. We didn't have staff to work in art or music, but we did have strong relations with people who were interested in the national power of New York to supply road shows and to give authentic advice anywhere outside of New York City. So we turned to an organization that had lapsed, not a very strong one at the time. It was called the National Theatre Conference. A professor named Edward C. Mabie, at the University of Iowa, was one of the leaders. He called the old members together and started a new program, which very quickly centered in Cleveland for central administration but had points of growth in all parts of the country.

GARD: Where did your interest in drama originate?

STEVENS: In my teaching days in Chicago. I worked with the Wrenn Collection on the North Shore, to create courses with critical texts of representative English plays of the seventeenth and eighteenth centuries. I went up to Wrenn's house to get my texts and made my own corrected texts from them for the printer. I brought out *Types of English Drama, 1660-1780* in 1923.

GARD: How did you find out he had them?

STEVENS: The chairman of our department at the University of Chicago, John Manly, worked steadily over several years in London on his Chaucer text. He got acquainted with Thomas J. Wise, who was known as a collector of rare books. He was a wealthy man. He had also been in touch with Mr. Wrenn, who had bought a great many rare seventeenth and eighteenth-century quartos. Out of that talk of Manly and Wise, I discovered where the books were, and I got to make my own copies for this anthology. I went to his house often throughout the winter and worked up texts for this first collection of material on the theatre in Britain between 1660 and 1780. I used it, of course, as a textbook.

GARD: So there had not been many classes in drama, as we are familiar with them today, in 1923?

STEVENS: No, there weren't many in this field. It wasn't long before Howard Mumford Jones and someone else had out a book similar to mine and had started a teaching system of considerable strength all through the country.

HOWARD MUMFORD JONES: *Plays of the Restoration and the 18th Century* developed out of two inciting causes. One was from the college representative of the publishers, who, while visiting Chapel Hill, thought he saw that such an anthology would be profitable because courses in the drama of the two periods seemed to him to be expanding over the country; and the other was the fact that Dougald MacMillan at Chapel Hill (the University of North Carolina) gave a course in the history of the drama, and I gave courses in the Restoration and the Eighteenth Century. Neither of us at the time could find a dramatic anthology that quite suited our needs. I am unable to recall the date of the Stevens anthology, but either we did not know about it or we found the collection rather more limited than the one we planned. Our anthology was, I think, somewhat fuller than Dave's, and we made something of a point of trying to give an eighteenth-century flavoring to our introductory essays on the several playwrights.

STEVENS: Developing a textbook in drama got me interested in the live theatre in America, and first of all in a man in Cleveland, who had heroically created a theatre tradition there and had two theatres running. We eventually helped him build a third one. Frederic McConnell was one of the first men who operated as a non-profit drama director, working in Cleveland and at a Chautauqua in New York State. Barclay Leathem was his comrade. They were leaders in management. Both had been in the National Theatre Conference from the beginning, had stayed through, and had become leaders in our programs during the war and steadily for twenty years throughout the country.

When I went to see McConnell in Cleveland, I started the program. I said, "You are the best man who has really done anything. Now what's your condition?" "Well," he said, "we're in trouble. We're thirty-seven thousand dollars in debt." I said, "We'll give you half if you can raise the other half." So he got the bill paid off in no time, and after that we helped him a considerable amount over many years.

GARD: Was there any connection between McConnell's theatre and Western Reserve University?

STEVENS: Yes, McConnell was running a community theatre, and Leathem was running the one in Western Reserve. So we helped both of them get on their feet and gave them the money to run the National Theatre Conference.

A good outcome of our work was in developing community drama in colleges and in communities, where we had very fine leaders. Through the National Theatre Conference many semi-professional and really professional friendships developed. Take, for example, the thing that Maxwell Anderson did. He gave the members of the Conference, some thirty directors, the right to produce locally, before national release, one of his new plays. We had him in meetings frequently. Brooks Atkinson also was a great friend of the National Theatre Conference. Atkinson and twenty of his professional friends came to a meeting at which he was given a citation by the Conference for what he had done for non-professional drama.

The lasting effects of the programs developed by the National Theatre Conference are too many to recall, but one clear statement I made is in a book for which I wrote an introduction to stories of ten leaders who had distinguished themselves in the years before 1950. The book was called *Ten Talents in the American Theatre.* One of the ten was Paul Green, who wrote fiction, folk stories, but above all outdoor play-pageants, on episodes in American history, called "symphonic dramas," which now total twenty-odd in number — many with very long summer runs at locations across the country.

Green was at the University of North Carolina, where he was doing his work in collaboration with Frederick Koch, director and playwright. Koch had studied at Harvard under George Pierce Baker. He ran the

Carolina Playmakers' theatre at the University of North Carolina twelve months a year for twenty years, developing young people who then became teachers, performers, or directors. Among his helpers and students were Paul Green and his wife, Elizabeth; Sam Selden, who became head of the drama school at the University of California at Los Angeles; and Josefina Niggli. On the twenty-fifth anniversary of the Carolina Playmakers, Koch brought together twenty-five national leaders in drama and theatre from across the country. Among the professionals was Clifford Odets. Another of those present was Alfred G. Arvold of North Dakota, creator of massive outdoor pageants. Koch had worked under his direction in North Dakota.

SAM SELDEN: When Professor Fred Koch left North Dakota in 1918 to accept a position in the English Department at the University of North Carolina, he was delighted with the opportunities offered him in the new engagement. Mr. Koch was passionately interested in discovering and exploiting native materials expressed in the imagery of theatre, and he set to work immediately to organize a group of students who would do something about it.

He trained his young people to compose plays about the life and history of the "folk people" who lived and labored in the fields and towns of the Piedmont country, up in the mountains, and along the coastal areas, and then gathered around those authors a few specialists in acting, directing, and the making of costumes and scenery, who would show the writers how to translate their literary figures into moving and speaking people on a stage.

Professor Koch's experimental native playmaking at the University of North Carolina quickly became successful. The creative writing and producing was presented in Chapel Hill, then taken around to schools, colleges, and towns of the state, then to other states, from Florida to Massachusetts. Everywhere the Carolina Folk Plays were seen, they caused excitement. Critics commented on them enthusiastically.

Even when the future of Professor Koch's productive experiment was hit, like so many other creative projects of the time, by the withering blight of the depression, it was saved by a sizeable grant from the Division for the Humanities of the Rockefeller Foundation. Dr. David Stevens had been watching the growth of Professor Koch's dramatic group and the effect it was having on both professional and educational experimental projects elsewhere. He felt that what it stood for should not be permitted to sink into oblivion. Through his vigorous efforts the grant was arranged, and the Playmakers went on to further healthy growth.

Out of the body of the Carolina Playmakers have come a number of stage authors — including a Pulitzer playwright — besides motion picture and television writers, biographers, and novelists. From them have come also professional actors, dancers, critics, producers, and teachers. One can't help wondering how much poorer some of America's media would have been today if they had not been nourished by the minds of the young men and women who were inspired by the enthusiasm and guidance of Professor Koch in their school days, and were given, at a critical period in their growth, a chance to complete their training by the alert assistance of Dr. Stevens through the foundation to which he was attached.

PAUL GREEN: I first met David Stevens by way of Professor Koch of the Carolina Playmakers. Mr. Koch had had some correspondence with different foundations, and he let me know one day that he had been asked to make application to the Rockefeller Foundation for help in his folk-play movement. He had ideas of help especially for talented people. Koch said, "Stevens has asked me to prepare an exhibit of work and to come up to New York and meet with him."

So we went to New York City, and I'll never forget the day. We waited a while and out came David Stevens. He was a tiny bit below medium height, but well-figured—a good strong, sinewy person. We went inside to his office, and Professor Koch got out his two big scrapbooks full of pictures. He started turning the pages, and Dr. Stevens called somebody in—I don't know if it was John Marshall or Chet D'Arms. Mr. Koch went on and on, and Stevens had already said that he would like to have us go to lunch.

The lunch hour came on and was passing, and I thought to myself, well, Mr. Koch, like the way he used to do his curtain talk before his plays, was again just overdoing it. It turned out that's exactly the kind of man Stevens was interested in, a man who was really an enthusiast, an idealist, and who forgot the world in favor of the ideas that possessed him. I don't remember how we ended the meeting, but ultimately Mr. Koch got a grant from the Rockefeller Foundation.

STEVENS: Another of these ten former fellows having the diversity of Paul Green was Robert Gard, now working in extension programs at the University of Wisconsin, but known first from his years of training players and writing and directing plays under Alexander Drummond, at Cornell University. From there he went to national success in Canada, for developing drama, local history, and folk materials at the University of Alberta. He had been asked to come to promote dramatic and historical studies of the past life of that Province. Through his efforts he inspired a whole area to bring in material and to start an archive on regional history. The people there had enough judgment and common sense to erect a building for housing local materials and to make this extension work in history, drama, and writing a permanent part of the regional program of their university. They did this so well that recently they have published a book of reports and studies and source materials that came out of his field work and that of his students. After those four successful years of establishing a provincial archive in its own building and a total program in drama and the arts at the University, he went to do further work for the Foundation. That brought him to the University of Wisconsin, where he has now stayed for many years.

Another story of regional service very closely related to this is one started with a good deal of our money in the state of Montana. Baker Brownell, of Northwestern University, was a teacher of philosophy who had written a great deal on what he thought to be the basic ingredient of American life and American character—the small community. Two or three of his books are still classics. Brownell and another man from Northwestern University, Dean Melby, performed a great service to the state of Montana by going there to develop among their four state institutions a single program for the arts, including drama and regional literature. Also, they had the idea that they were to have one administrator to end the rivalry of these four institutions, to control the budgets, and to limit the types of labor and the duties of various professors.

Well, this project went on beautifully for a while and had some unusual results. In one little town, Darby, they reorganized all community activities. It was a ghost town, almost, and had not found a way to keep its young people there or to endear the town to the people. One of its weaknesses was that the town was a political haven. There were nineteen county and state-paid officers living in Darby, traveling out of there all over the state and not doing anything for anybody at home, except to make local talks now and then on agriculture and farming. With the cooperation of the local industry, Brownell and Melby organized the project and ran it with a community director in Darby, and so brought back to the town many of its young people. The town has prospered moderately ever since. There were two or three other men in the state who became extremely valuable to Montana, with the help of Brownell. One man, Joseph Kinsey Howard, spent his entire life in the state working on historical themes in news writing and produced a classic work, his *Montana Margins,* brilliant accounts of life in his state.

Another example of lively action was at the Seattle Playhouse, which was one of the strong, outlying operating companies. It was under the direction of Burton James and his wife, Florence. One of his helpers was a man who is still active in New York theatre, Albert M. Ottenheimer. He is the actor who had the role of a druggist in "West Side Story" and played it thousands of times. He and his wife are still living and acting in New York. Well, this Seattle Playhouse was a pioneer in many ways. For example, we had Ottenheimer go through the high school systems to give talks on Shakespeare and at all stops put on plays with a traveling company.

ALBERT M. OTTENHEIMER: I was one of the co-founders, with the late Burton W. James and (still living) Florence B. James, of the Seattle Repertory Playhouse in 1928, and remained with the theatre as actor, press representative, head of sales, and one of its business managers for a period of twenty years. During the period of the Washington State Theatre (funded by the Rockefeller Foundation Division of the Humanities under Dr. Stevens' aegis), 1936-39, in addition to being involved in its direction and management, I served as advance man for most of its productions; one phase of that work was to speak at assemblies in advance of each production, in which capacity I made hundreds of such speeches and spoke to literally tens of thousands of high school, junior high school, and (in some instances) elementary school students. I ought to mention that I wrote the prospectus for the Washington State Theatre project, which won the Rockefeller Foundation grant, and wrote all the reports of the W.S.T. to the Foundation.

STEVENS: Of the important men who developed future leaders, I named Koch; there was also Mabie, of the University of Iowa, whose driving energy and talent made his share in the National Theatre Conference important for twenty-five years. One of the older men, who was really the bellwether in all early work in university drama was Alexander Drummond, of Cornell University, who produced plays written by his own students and who inspired younger men, as he did when he sent Gard to see if he could get a fellowship. I would have given Gard a fellowship, aside from his own qualifications, on the single recommendation of Alexander Drummond, who had more prestige as a director of college theatre than any other man of his generation.
GARD: In other words, with experience you were able to develop a rapport with many of the men at the top of their fields?
STEVENS: For example, with Alexander Drummond, once we knew how good he was, we gave him money to help him do what he wanted—training people and getting men to write. He was one of the few men who repre-

sented fine quality in the field of drama at a place to send a student to get training. Gilmor Brown, at Pasadena, was another. There were five or six centers where we could back people and know we would get excellent returns.

JOHN PARKER: One of the interesting things about Dr. Stevens was that he gave mostly small stipends, and for the most part because of specialized talents of individuals. When he would select another recipient, he very wisely, I thought, sent him to one of many centers across the United States and said, as an example, "Go to Chapel Hill among other places, and see what they are doing or planning to do, and it will help you with whatever project you have." They did. These were people from England, from Canada, from Ireland. They would always come here for a few weeks to kind of catch the spirit, if we had the right spirit.

My own involvement with Dr. Stevens began when I came down to Chapel Hill and met him in Professor Koch's office. I had been teaching the dramatic arts in high school, and I had just produced a play that I had written here under Mr. Koch's direction, following his instructions to his beginning playwrights. He always said, "Write about what you know best," and I thought I knew the black situation in eastern North Carolina better than I knew anything else; at least, it was the one thing that had impressed me up to that point. So I wrote a full-length play of the black people in my neighborhood.

Well, this play was a success, and afterwards I was invited to come back to work here where I had my undergraduate training. My work was primarily in the capacity of spreading the gospel over the state and trying to drum up and polish up some of the dramatic interests, not only in the secondary schools, but in the colleges and the community groups all over North Carolina.

Dr. Stevens was a sterling taskmaster and a very good businessman. He always insisted on getting periodic reports on how you were doing. He further insisted that the university, in accepting generosity from the Foundation he represented, also make a contribution in each of these regards. And that's the reason I stayed on here at the University of North Carolina. President Graham and Professor Koch, in putting me to work, had to give some guarantee that the University was going to carry on with my salary after this two-year Rockefeller grant gave out. They honored that commitment, and the stipend which Mr. Stevens gave in this particular case I thought was very generous. The University gave me an opportunity to supplement that income by going out and teaching university courses for credit in various centers about the state. That's how I made my living for the first two years.

STEVENS: There were several professional men in theatre who supported academic and community work in playmaking, such as George Freedley, of the New York Public Library, as writer of reviews and articles for the National Theatre Conference *Bulletin,* and Barrett Clark, editor of play texts for Dramatists Play Service, who obtained copies of plays for rental use as soon as the Broadway runs ended. Margo Jones, with her theatre in Dallas on a year-around schedule, read countless manuscripts of known and new authors, and brought Tennessee Williams to notice and eventual high place as playwright. She also produced professionally on Broadway. Norris Houghton, working in New York, brought national and metropolitan streams of play production into relationship by his reviews and direction, while others recorded in this biographical accounting created their own publics in their own playhouses across the country.

Two examples of how the Foundation gave specific aid to individuals through several years can be seen in the work of Leslie Cheek and Gilmor Brown. Leslie Cheek left William and Mary College after creating a well-rounded department in the arts—historically taught and creatively practiced — in drama through all essentials, from the writing to acting and staging plays, in studio and classroom and museum decor. He went on to the municipal art gallery of Baltimore, which was patronized by wealthy families and benefited by loans of paintings from homes of the old families for special occasions.

Leslie took advantage of a real chance by proposing an exhibit with fine modern and old gilt-framed paintings. This he paralleled later on the road with his novel travelling art show, in the state-owned mobile truck, that moved throughout the state all year. He began the first year with loaned gilt-framed old paintings, then with both old and modern, and so on into varied new approaches. There, as at Williamsburg, he created something that endures, going on to make the state gallery in Richmond the finest for variety and excellence. The theatre attached to the museum was a gift of the Foundation.

Typical in regional influence was Gilmor Brown, at the Pasadena Playhouse, with three stages and a large school. Although he did a great deal of work with Hollywood, and may have wasted some of his time, Gilmor Brown for a generation ably ran a self-supporting stage and school. He also ran what he called his Play Box, for new plays and plays that would not have commercial appeal, in order to develop writers and actors.

GARD: Did you give the Pasadena Playhouse any financial support?

STEVENS: Yes; fellowships, constantly.

GARD: I wonder if you could say a word about the fellowship program as it was operated in theatre arts.

STEVENS: Through the National Theatre Conference and directly, we supported drama by awards to men and women who were very near to finishing first-rate pieces of manuscript; and these would have try-outs, as they did at Pasadena, all through the Conference. Grants were also made to playwrights as resident writers attached to theatres to teach, write, and train young writers.

GARD: You thought the fellowship program had great value in extending the potential, the talent, the horizons of these young writers.

STEVENS: The one I didn't say enough about was Margo Jones and her theatre, which was run on a shoestring. They didn't have much money, but they had the backing of the city of Dallas. Margo Jones told me she thought she had read more manuscripts than any other person in her generation. She was reading new plays all the time, in order to give many their first production in her Dallas theatre.

Margo deserves a descriptive sentence or two. She had heavy brown hair and was a medium-sized woman, physically strong, able to take a lot of hard work. I was in Dallas with my wife one time, and we went out to see one of her plays. After the play she asked us to come to her room to meet some of her actors. We sat around, some of us on the floor, late into the night, talking about drama. This was typical of her drive and enthusiasm.

GARD: You gave a fellowship to a young Mexican woman, Josefina Niggli, who did some good work for you.

STEVENS: She was a very talented writer whose subject was her own people. She wrote both plays and books. One was a series of short stories that Hollywood purchased. Josefina came in 1950 to see us at Pasadena, when I was working at the Huntington Library. She had been in Hollywood for several weeks, working on a production of an elaborate Mexican play, based on her book of short stories. She was getting fifteen hundred dollars a week. She stayed there for six months, then went back to teaching and writing in North Carolina.

She had a great sense of American folklore and of Mexican people and their history. One time she took a whole year off to become a professional photographer. She went back to her girlhood home, Monterey, took scores of pictures, and then wrote her book about Monterey, entitled *Step Down, Elder Brother*, addressed to the Spanish occupants of her country at the time the Spanish landlords were being dispossessed and the free spirit of Mexico was beginning to appear. A remarkable novel.

JOSEFINA NIGGLI: David didn't think in terms of specialties. One time he was talking about Ireland to me and what a great country it was. When I said I'd never been there, he asked if I'd like to go. Naturally I said yes, and really forgot it, because I thought his comment was just one of those things people say. (Knowing David as well as I do, I should have known better!) The next thing I knew I had a traveling fellowship to Dublin and London and was on my way. When I stopped off in New York, a friend took me to lunch. He said, "Just why do you have this fellowship, Miss Niggli?" I shrugged my shoulders wanting to say, "Because David wants me to have it." I did say, "I don't know exactly." Anyway, when I came back, I happened to mention this to David as a funny incident. He didn't think it was funny at all. He said, "It was time for you to absorb the poetry of Ireland." And that, I think, was his greatest gift, that ability to feel the need of a person.

II. The Depression and World War II

GARD: Were you conscious of the times, especially in the 1930's, of the depression, or the deprived state of people and their inability to pay much money to see theatre or music? Did this have any bearing on the kinds of things you were doing?

STEVENS: I don't think so. I think we did realize that these community theatre and university theatre programs were satisfying a natural desire of people, and in many of our other programs we assumed that the people wanted them. So I don't think it ever bothered, because we knew what we were going to work in.

I think it's an easy summary to say that every Christmas, at the trustee meetings, we defined what our aims were to be. We might run a program for five or ten or fifteen years, but we decided on renewing it every year, partly as protection. Even in an exceptional case, we didn't go outside our field. No, I don't think the depression affected the work of the Foundation, except for the increased number of applications.

And it's so important not to be trapped by a pile of paper. As one example, the Ford Foundation was finally ready to start active work in the late 1950's on the arts, and my old helper, Chet D'Arms, went over to the Ford Foundation. He and McNeil Lowry, vice-president for the Arts of the Ford Foundation, found a big stack of applications on each of their desks. Some of the trustees were impatient for some of their friends who had applied. They said to D'Arms, "Get that application from Mr. X out and look it over." He said, "No, we won't touch it." He and Lowry took a whole year to travel the country and make up their minds what they were going to support. They didn't touch any of that old paper work. That's the way you have to do it. You can't become fragmented into projects you can't possibly follow up.

In music and art we never did much, because we had too much to do and too little money.

GARD: You evidently didn't lose any sleep over the fact that you were not getting into music and art.

STEVENS: We didn't do anything. John D., III, who is pilot of the family nowadays, and creator of the Lincoln Center, would have been pleased to have us do much more than we did; but the only thing we gave in any amount was to the Museum of Modern Art, where we created the film archive to preserve the history of the motion picture.

GARD: I want to get back to the depression for a moment. You let the Federal Theatre take care of employment for actors and that kind of thing? You weren't really concerned with furnishing jobs for actors?

STEVENS: No, we didn't put money on a man with a fellowship unless we knew he would have a job and could go somewhere and do something. There was no subsidy of people because they needed it; the Federal Government did it through W.P.A. under Harry Hopkins and Hallie Flanagan, and a few of the people who were close to the war program. We certainly salvaged a lot of people who needed help, some who were actors, perhaps; but it was always on our test of certain employment or individual advance in some service after our support.

GARD: In your work, did you try consciously to keep the whole country in mind?

STEVENS: No.

GARD: You picked out this place or that place, or this man or that man, and you gave in relation to—

STEVENS: —individuals, or places where we were germinating a new program, as in Chinese, Japanese, and Russian — or in drama, or in history.

GARD: But you didn't necessarily pick it out geographically?

STEVENS: Not really. Naturally we worked where there was a need. Of course, the big salvage job that we did was with Jewish professors driven out of Germany. Humanities brought some hundred and thirty of those men to America, and as one widespread effect strengthened the whole field of philosophy. We brought over art critics and teachers like Erwin Panofsky to Princeton, and religious-philosophical historians like Paul Tillich, who went to Columbia, and some remarkable older professors of classics, one of whom, Alexander Turyn, went to the University of Michigan. He classified materials for research studies in Latin and published definitive studies on Vatican manuscripts of Latin classics.

GARD: Where did the idea of helping displaced scholars, mostly German Jews, originate?

STEVENS: It came from a sense of social duty and of common sense, to use great possibilities of developing American scholarship; but it was also related to the human task of rescuing great individual abilities that were going to be destroyed by assassination.

GARD: So the Foundation provided for transportation and resettlement?

STEVENS: We had men in Europe finding them and getting them out, and we paid for their coming over, and paid in many cases up to seven years for their salaries in universities where they were distributed. We found their wives and children and brought them together, too.

GARD: David, what was your reaction when the war broke out?

STEVENS: I got my reaction in the Netherlands, where I was when the war broke out. I was able to get away on a ship to Norway and get home. We knew the thing was coming, of course. In one way the war gave great opportunity for use of philanthropy. I think most of these programs got their big push, and some of them would never have had such a good growth as they did had not the war forced people into new kinds of creative research, and as with drama, into some help to thousands and hundreds of thousands of men who were abroad and idle when not fighting. The drama program was broken wide open by the war in this country as well.

Very soon, in 1940 I think, we began to develop men who went with the troops abroad in the Second World War to form acting companies for uninterrupted production at Army bases. I remember one time we had over twenty members of the National Theatre Conference, nearly half of the membership, abroad, working with the troops, taking men out of the camps, training them, having them put on stage productions.

Even after the war our work continued. I was in Fort Meade, near Washington, with Barclay Leathem during a training program for overseas duty. With us was Charles Judd, formerly director of the School of Education at the University of Chicago, who was at that time the head of training for all aspects of the Army educational program being developed for after-war engagement of interest among the armies. In that stay we were living next to the barbed-wire enclosures housing several hundred German Army officers held there and shortly to be repatriated to East Germany. Among these were many Russians who had gone into the German Army as a way to help their own country through a hoped-for end of its tyranny. All these Russians killed themselves. To be repatriated would have meant the same end under far more distressing circumstances. That trip into Fort Meade, with Judd and Barclay Leathem, was representative of what the universities, and particularly the men we had helped develop in drama, did for the war effort.

BARCLAY LEATHEM: The Washington episode that I recall preceded David Stevens' visit to Fort Meade. It had to do with efforts to give enlisted men the opportunity to provide their own entertainment by putting on plays. It was not easy. Commanding officers rightly were concerned with training men for combat, not for careers as actors. David thought it would help if we could get through to the President and asked Paul Green, who knew Mrs. Roosevelt personally, to arrange a meeting with her. He did and the four of us, David, Paul Green, Barrett H. Clark and I met in Washington the day before Thanksgiving in 1940 and prepared a statement explaining our belief that not all men in the armed services were interested in athletics as a means of recreation during their free time—that some might want to put on plays, even to write their own.

I remember the reaction of the cab driver when we said, "The White House." He looked us over and replied, "For an extra dollar I can take you to Washington's Monument and the Lincoln Memorial." We assured him we were expected. When we arrived we were ushered into the Red Room and soon Mrs. Roosevelt joined us. She was a gracious lady, and after listening to our story she said, "I like your proposal and will read it to the President tomorrow as we drive to Hyde Park for our Thanksgiving dinner." It was not long thereafter that the War Department, acting through the Special Services branch, accepted our experimental plan to appoint a civilian theatre director in each of the corps areas to organize the project that became known as Soldier Shows. David financed the plan through the Rockefeller Foundation. After it succeeded the War Department took it over and it is still in effect as the Army Theatre Arts Association.

STEVENS: A book by Hallie Flanagan, *Arena,* summed up results from the Second World War from Federal spending on the arts under the Works Progress Administration, headed by Harry Hopkins and sponsored by Mrs. Roosevelt. Drama was benefited because aid to professional theatre people brought them directly into the playmaking of the people in every part of the nation. The Federal Writers Project state guide books brought out local values for artists, writers, and playwrights. Artists were commissioned for murals in post offices and schools as well.

As for our language programs, which we had initiated ahead of others, and so were far ahead of the government and partly the universities, the war was the thing that gave impulse and variety of outlet in the various languages and led to what they call today area programs. All of this really put America on the way in its present effort to try to become a civilized world power and to do things rather than fight.

GARD: Did the length of the war sometimes lead to a sense of discouragement?

STEVENS: When you are talking about helping, just because there is less opportunity doesn't mean that you don't get as much done as you can with so much money and so much time. It didn't, as far as I know, change the pace of the Foundation in what it was up to. It went ahead on things that it thought were emergent opportunities. Take men like Alan Gregg, who went through the war as a surgeon in Europe. He came home and went to work for the Foundation, of course, and that background of his in the European war gave him a strong impulse to do certain things that perhaps wouldn't have come except through the war. That's certainly true of all our plans of helping graduate work in languages and cultures. It's always true, of course, that you can't do as much as you want to do. When we had a program, we determined what we were going to work at, and we did the best we could in that field.

III. Film and Theatre

GARD: One of the things that you did get into in the creative arts was a program with the Museum of Modern Art. Could you elaborate on that?

STEVENS: Related to the establishment of centers for staged plays was the saving for lasting record and constant use of our motion picture films. The film library of the Museum of Modern Art was wholly created by the Division for the Humanities, under John Abbott and his English wife, Iris Barry. She had wide experience in film before coming across to Hollywood, where her experiences prepared her for the plan to bring into safe storage, for continuing use, the films of all the leading actors and directors of early years, down to the middle of the century.

To launch the plan the Museum sent Abbott to Princeton, New Jersey, on the night Erwin Panofsky, German art critic and great friend of film makers here and abroad, was to speak. When John came home from this Princeton conference, he came out of the Hudson tunnel and heard a police whistle; then he realized he was in New York, his driver's license was in his home town in Maryland, and he was driving his wife's car with a California license. The officer told him that when he came out of the tunnel he had failed to turn on his lights.

Then the policeman quizzed him a long time through the window, and finally he said, "I think I'll get in and talk to you a while." So he climbed into the car and sat down. Finally John realized that this man knew something about the early business of film when he said, "You know, they were making films on Long Island, and I was a super in those early films. Finally they moved the whole outfit to California, and my good Irish mother wouldn't allow me to go with those evil people. So here I am a flatfoot in New York, and most of my friends made a lot of money." He said, "Now John, I've got you on seven violations of city ordinances. But I'll tear up my tickets and even escort you home if you'll let me come up to the Museum and see some of those old films." So he did, and very often he would stop a film to say, "Look! There I am. You can see where I was in that particular film"—one of a crowd of extras working on location in Long Island years before.

As I have tried to explain quickly, these things happened for staged plays and film because the scene was ready for development in regional drama, and for saving the examples of the art of silent films as history. The great performers and directors are for all time in the record and on the screens across the country, under rental, every week of the year at the Museum of Modern Art in New York City.

One of our unusual men, George Izenour, was working in a W.P.A. theatre under Hallie Flanagan at the Exposition in San Francisco, staging plays on Treasure Island. After leaving college, he worked on engineering for stage purposes, and had developed a theatre in his own Ohio college. He was basically an engineer and inventor. We started George Izenour on his great career as designer. Very soon he was located at Yale University, with a sizeable grant to stay until he developed his new system of theatre lighting, using the photoelectric cell. Then he went on to design and to build, up to the present time, some eighty-five theatres in the United States. Out of that one man, then, we got a network of modern buildings all over the country backed by local people who no longer had road shows and who wanted theatre.

Izenour is now at Yale as professor in the Drama School. The University has given him an elaborate installation of machines and whatever else is needed for his laboratory of theatre design and for building essential elements. His creative laboratory is unlike any other. George's next project is to secure an endowment of a million dollars as security for all his drawings and the machinery, and for salaries of others after he ends work.

At Yale we had a man who worked with Izenour when he was working on his lighting research — Allardyce Nicoll, the famous director of drama in England. He came over and took over the Yale Theatre, as director for the drama school. He brought with him a prominent German historian of the theatre, Alois M. Nagler, who is still there. Nicoll made Yale a scholarly and creative school and then returned eventually to England.

ALOIS M. NAGLER: Hallie Flanagan, then director of the Federal Theatre project, spotted a poor Austrian immigrant with a distinguished

European career in theatre. Amidst a nationwide depression he was struggling to find a niche in academia. She put me in contact with Dr. David Stevens, who, with innate human kindness and uncanny instinct for potentials, suggested that with the help of a Rockefeller stipend I move to Yale in order to finish a research project on theatre audiences.

Allardyce Nicoll, chairman of the Department of Drama at Yale, agreed to my presence at Yale as a Rockefeller research fellow. He eventually resigned and returned to his native England, which opened the channel for me, and I have been teaching Nicoll's courses for the past thirty years. In short, I would not have had this career without Dr. Stevens' guidance. No doubt, another Rockefeller investment which paid off.

STEVENS: Why was it important that these things happened? As I tried to say quickly, we energized the communities and the universities and colleges at the time that road plays were dropping out. We developed a lot of people, did work in the service of the Army here and abroad, in the training camps of the United States, and in colleges and communities. As with Paul Green, we aided many other present-day leaders in theatre. One example is Christian Moe, who now runs a big program at Southern Illinois University.

CHRISTIAN MOE: I recall meeting David Stevens for the first time when he visited me at the University of North Carolina in Chapel Hill in 1955. He struck me at once as being extremely good-humored, warmhearted, and very knowledgeable about the theatre. And, as a lowly graduate student, I was flattered that this immaculately dressed man with a twinkle in both eyes took a genuine interest in the concerns of a mere student. Learning of my interest in playwriting and historical drama, he remarked directly, "You ought to meet Paul Green face to face. I'm going to his home tonight. You come along." I did so. It was a delightful evening. Paul Green talked of writing problems he was having with *The Founders* (a drama about the Jamestown colony presented in 1957), and later he seated us in a ring and conducted what amounted to a fascinating seminar on Eugene O'Neill, to which we all contributed. This was heady company and conversation for a student in those days. And I never forgot Stevens' kindness in letting me be a part of it. "Hearing Paul Green hold court is an education in itself," commented Stevens as he drove me home. "You won't forget it." I didn't.

On another occasion several years later, I had another reason to be grateful to David Stevens. With my collaborator, I had sent a prospectus of a book about historical drama to the publisher of a university press. Receiving the unidentified readers' comments, I recognized one as from the hand of Mr. Stevens. The comment to the publisher read, "I know these guys and they can do it. Just put the screws on them hard so they'll come out with a good book." The advice was accepted apparently—right down the line.

STEVENS: Today, qualified directors in the regional centers are working with people engaged in the performing arts across the entire country. A few of the more important centers, because of design and full effect on our environment, are those at Harvard University; the Community Center at Akron, Ohio; the Performing Arts Center in Milwaukee; the Jesse Jones Memorial and the Alley Theatre in Dallas; the structure at Tempe, Arizona, designed in part by Frank Lloyd Wright; the Community House at Albuquerque, New Mexico; and an unusual one lately opened in El Paso, Texas.

These are all shown in George Izenour's forthcoming book, which is to be a monumental record of theatre structures across Europe, and east to Tel Aviv, on both shores of the Mediterranean, across the Atlantic, and over this country from coast to coast. The nine hundred pages of text with over six hundred illustrations are a product of many years of travel to sites so that the measurement might be recorded for every structure in exact proportion to that of all, from the Colosseum to the smallest one known. So the regional theatres are now housing plays across the country, in many cases far more adequately than in large cities or on Broadway. The eighty-odd new houses across the United States for all forms of staged presentation—ballet, opera, music, and large spectacles as well as plays—are out there because of the engineering and imaginative design of George C. Izenour, one of our fellows.

GEORGE C. IZENOUR: I met David Stevens when I was working in Federal Theatre in California. I had just designed my first theatre, and he appeared on the scene and asked to see this theatre. He wanted me to explain to him how it operated, which I proceeded to do as best I could. He took all this in, saying very little; and at the end of our first conversation he said, "Young man, I want you to write me a letter and tell me what you want to do." I promptly did that, and the upshot of the letter was that he came back to me with a letter and said, "You're the kind of person who ought to be doing research in this field." "Well," I said, "that's wonderful, but how do you do this?" He said, "I can't tell you how, but I can give you a fellowship for a year and perhaps you can find out."

I was notified on July 1, 1939, that I had been made a fellow of the Rockefeller Foundation to travel across the country with my wife to visit universities that had departments of drama. I stopped at Northwestern, Carnegie Tech, which is now Carnegie-Mellon, and finally at Yale. The only reason I landed at Yale was that Yale had an unused squash court, which they were willing to give over to a young man who had a fellowship from the Rockefeller Foundation and who wanted to do research. The first nine months of the fellowship at Yale produced a working model, from which later became the first all-electronic dimming system for theatre lighting. This fellowship brought a three-year research grant which was then to be carried out in the laboratory, which now had a foothold at Yale.

After the war I had some exceedingly lean years, let us say, until Stevens happened one day to come in on me, having done other business on the Yale campus. Without asking any questions whatever, he said, "I'm going to send you on a lecture tour." He then proceeded to line up for me lectures at Northwestern, the University of Wisconsin, Carnegie Tech, and the Case School of Applied Science. He offered this small stipend in the hope that the work I had done at Yale might provide a stimulus to someone else, and that's exactly what happened; the lecture at the Goodman Theatre in Chicago produced a very avid listener in Maurice Niessen, who within two months commissioned me to build a second system like the one that had first been installed at Yale three years previously.

This system, as they say in the business, was built entirely with a file and a hand-ax in the laboratory at Yale, and in succeeding years I produced systems at Carnegie Tech and the University of Delaware. This was enough to bring on commercial recognition. In the meantime I had succeeded in obtaining patents to protect this thing. These patents were licensed commercially. I then began to put back into the laboratory a portion of those royalties, which eventually made the laboratory self-sustaining.

What David Stevens did throughout the four years that he supported me at Yale, plus the original one-year Foundation grant as a fellow, was to provide me a chance to think at a crucial time of my life. Without that, I know that things would have turned out much differently. I think his real strength was the ability to ask the right question. He had a unique way to get next to a person. It was not only his penetrating question, but his penetrating look. You just knew that you couldn't fail this man.

STEVENS: One story outside the narrative of the American theatre is from an incident during a stay in England. In London I met Tyrone Guthrie, who then was just coming into prominence as a director and creative figure in all aspects of theatre. I had tea at his very small apartment, along with an equally interesting man named Nevill Coghill, who had his base of production at a theatre in Oxford and who taught in the University. Talk was on the community and university theatres of Great Britain, of the support from the Arts Council, and of our similar work under funds of the Rockefeller Foundation in this country. Our initiative through the National Theatre Conference brought to print a monograph used in the campaign later on to bring Guthrie to the United States. The theatre in Minneapolis bearing his name is now a lasting evidence of the spirit of the city of Minneapolis as well as admirable proof of the way this country can become nationally active in all the arts when conditions are right for action leading to steady support.

8. AFTER WORLD WAR II

I. Japan and England

GARD: What projects were you involved in after World War II, David?
STEVENS: First, let me tell you of an assignment I got through my position in the Foundation. I was one of twenty-four American educators taken to Japan in 1946 to draft fresh programs of educational service. The Japanese had some strong research men in specialized fields, but their education was traditional, on their own historic basis; and it was so intensive that it was discouraging to hope for a job where there were far more people than could possibly find jobs in the field. They drove their children, from childhood, to pass examinations and be ready.

When the Army moved into Japan, it needed some advice on how to remake the total system of education of a nation emerging from a medieval system with all the undemocratic controls of a samurai society. It had a committee here pick out twenty-four people, and we were there for a month working with Japanese specialists, finally writing a modified Japanese-American program of popular education that included everything, of course, from kindergarten up through the graduate school and research work.

For the first week, every day we had a morning session where prominent Japanese educators talked of their areas of work. There were a great many Japanese professors there, and some Army men. We quickly broke up into units to handle various aspects of education. The third week of the visit, we were told to get our reports ready, and we were to start a series of night sessions at which time each unit would read its report for criticism. My share was in writing the report for higher education up through graduate and professional schools.

This went on actively and successfully. We finally got to the group of four dealing with teacher training. As we listened, it was very evident that we were getting a complete picture—but it was an American picture. It was obvious to all of us that their attitude toward education was built on the American system. When it was finished, no one spoke until the most courageous, Charles Johnson, the president of Fisk University, said, "That report could have been written just as well in Morningside Heights without a visit to Japan."

GARD: Was there as a result of your work a drastic change in the way these children were to be educated?

STEVENS: I don't know. I know what we prescribed, and I have a copy of the program we wrote. We were pioneering. I hope that the effect from our report appears in textbooks, teacher training, popular reading, and reforms politically and socially.

GARD: You didn't worry too much that you were doing something that might backfire?

STEVENS: It couldn't backfire as long as the American Army was there. They could draw up this program and cooperate with the Japanese leaders and try to change their attitudes toward each other and toward ideas. The theories of higher education and secondary education that had grown in America were to be adapted in many ways by the Japanese.

One incident in our month-long visit was being received by the Emperor, who asked what chance he had to get a good teacher for the prince. We got the teacher for him, and this had a long-range effect on the education of the Japanese people. And there were missionaries, remember, and the YMCA, which had worked in Japan for years. We applied some of our ideas through what they were able to do. These people became makers of new textbooks, and they won the cooperation of the Japanese people. We were partially able to do the same thing in Korea. I met men in Japan who went back to Korea and entered into full-time university work. They had the same problems.

The other program I was going to mention was that to help humanists after the war. A lot of our finest men had gone into service from the universities; so we brought Donald Goodchild, an officer of the American Council of Learned Societies, to help us for a year on a national study of humanists in the Second World War. We thought to provide three thousand dollars apiece for a hundred men, and we allotted that money on recommendations from Goodchild.

One of them received notice on his birthday in a trench on Okinawa; another man didn't learn of his award until he got off the boat in New

York. He had been a prisoner in a German camp but had escaped. Somehow he got back to New York, where on arrival at the dock his family told him, "You don't need to worry. You have promise of enough money to help you get started again."

JOHN S. DIEKHOFF: The Foundation had to seek the post-war fellows out. Young humanists in armed forces scattered throughout the world would not read notices of fellowships available nor be able to apply for them. Accordingly, I gather, David Stevens and his colleagues asked senior scholars to make nominations and the fellows were chosen on the basis of those recommendations.

I was in the Pentagon in the office of the director of Military Training when the Foundation representative came to see me. He began the interview by asking me what scholarly activity I would be engaged in if I were not in the Army.

Not long before I entered the Army I had finished a book on *Paradise Lost,* not published until 1946 because of the paper shortage. I told him about that and about a book I wanted to write on Defoe. We talked about Defoe at some length. I think I was asked to send an outline of the projected book, and I think I did. I am not sure.

Some time later I got a letter from the Foundation telling me that I had not been selected for a fellowship. A few weeks after that I received another letter telling me that there had been so many good candidates that the Foundation was increasing its appropriation for the humanities post-war fellowships and that I was among those added to the first list. That was a good letter to get!

After the war, I went to see David Stevens and John Marshall—there was a third Foundation officer in the conference, too, but I have forgotten who he was. My purpose was to ask permission to change my project from a book on Defoe to a book on municipal colleges. Stevens had seen my book on *Paradise Lost* and of course my earlier book, *Milton on Himself,* and he said complimentary things about them. He would have preferred another literary piece from me, I think. Someone—teasing me, I suspect —said that education was not in the Division for the Humanities and that a book about education could not qualify. I argued that education is a humane discipline and that humanists should be concerned with educational problems. I think there was no real doubt that the Foundation officers would approve my project, but we had a spirited, leisurely conversation. Busy men were generous with their time. In the end, I think it was Stevens who said, "Look, Diekhoff, we gave the fellowship to you, not to Defoe. Of course you must write what you want to write."

I spent the academic year 1948-49 writing *Democracy's College*. How can I tell what difference the fellowship made? I might have written *Democracy's College* anyway, or something like it. And I might not have written it. The point of the program was that it was for the likes of me. It was extremely important to me and David Stevens knew it.

STEVENS: We gave two of these awards to men at Princeton, Professors Mike Oates, a classicist, and Francis R. Godolphin, a historian. Out of their interest in what it had done for them, and from their concern for higher education, as for research in the humanities, they later were able to establish at Princeton the Woodrow Wilson Fellowships by raising private funds. This system of giving award fellowships for advanced men became the Woodrow Wilson National Scholarships funded by the United States Government.

1946 was an exceptional year. I mentioned earlier that the Foundation had occasion to make large single grants for special projects. A very important one was completed in that year, the Bodleian Library extension. On many of my visits to Oxford I discussed other humanistic matters with the secretary of the Clarendon Press, Kenneth Sisam. He acted as our agent in a limited program to subsidize authors — especially displaced Germans — in finishing manuscripts. In one visit immediately after the war, he told me what had happened to the Press' stock of books during the war as the entire Press had been taken over by the government for war needs in printing. Their famous little series called Oxford Classics, little blue books — there must be one hundred fifty titles — were so badly depleted in stock of prime numbers that Sisam said that at a good rate of progress, with other things, it would take many years to get the stock back in shape. He didn't feel too optimistic about how long it would take. He showed me all the empty rooms in the warehouses.

Now on the Bodleian. Sisam was one of the men brought over by the Rockefeller Foundation when Selskaar Gunn, of the Paris office, and I had developed the beginnings of a project that turned out to be the largest single one in the humanities program. At the end of negotiations the Foundation agreed to provide sixty per cent of the cost of a very large and necessary addition to the Bodleian Library.

We brought over Sisam in a delegation of ten men, and they traveled all over America, seeing big libraries and getting their eyes opened to what they had to do, in a way they hadn't known before. Also, these men were picked out by Oxford University because they represented opposing sides of the argument as to where the library should go. Some people wanted it put on the edge of the city, to make it only a storehouse. After a good deal of argument, it was settled to build it across the road from the old Bodleian, with a passage for book carriers underground to serve the big reading room of the Bodleian. It was finished in 1946.

One great change was needed to aid the readers in the colleges at the Bodleian as at the British Museum in London. You see, they didn't use card catalogs, only little slips pasted in books. It was impossible to keep those records up and to make slips in a reasonable time as the new books appeared. There was very little data on the book slips. Among the provisions we put into the project was that they should consider the flexibility of a card system for Oxford and the British Museum.

This trip of the Bodleian Commission, which took a good deal of time, and a good deal of money, brought things together. The only final argument I met was when the rector of the year, the head of Lincoln College, had me at his quarters for lunch. In the large hall he had put up thirty or forty pictures of Oxford, to show the skyline and how it had never been changed. He wished to persuade me to say something about limiting the height of the new building for the Bodleian in order to preserve the amenities. I wouldn't say anything, of course.

On one of these visits, at All Soul's College — that most prestigious college — they did such things for me as to have me sit next to T. S. Eliot at dinner. Of that I can remember nothing, except that I sat beside him at dinner.

Ruth and I came to London to attend the dedication, and we stayed in the Mitre Hotel, in the rooms reserved for royal visits. They did everything they could to make us feel we were part of the University. The morning before the dedication, we were taken to a very large room in All Soul's. About forty of us were arranged in a circle; then the Queen came by and shook hands with all of us. I remember she asked me if I had had a good crossing. I presume the only apt remark I made the whole time at Oxford was to say, "Yes, an excellent crossing, on a ship named the Queen Mary." And then the King greeted us. The rest of that morning was spent in a rehearsal of the actual procession for the opening of the door of the library. Some of the royal party did not get to the rehearsal, which had a little effect on the procession later.

That night I was taken to dinner with the chancellors of all the universities of Britain. I sat next to Lord Halifax. Ruth and I knew him and his wife, because we had been entertained at the embassy in Washington. The Oxford meeting for dinner was very agreeable. There was wonderful chatter, most of it in "Oxford pidgin-English" I would call it, which I could understand partly. That was the evening before the luncheon we had on the day of the dedication at one of the large college halls.

At this luncheon there was a dais with about twenty of us at one end of a great hall. I was on one end of the string, facing the architect who had designed the building. He showed me a little key in a velvet box and said, "Here's the key we are going to use to open the door." I looked at it and saw it was a beautiful silver key with a filigreed handle. I said to him, "I think, Sir Giles, I would leave that door unlocked." "Oh," he said, "that key is not only beautiful, but it is efficient."

Well, we went to the ceremony, held in the old Sheldonian Theatre, which is built with very high-pitched seats. It is a circular building, and on the side of the speaker has a high bank of benches. It must have been an angle of fifty degrees going up those steps. As we came into the hall, the secretary of the University, Mr. Veale, was behind me. In front of me was the lady-in-waiting, who hadn't been at the rehearsal. She was walking with her partner in the royal party, just ahead of me.

As we started into the Sheldonian, Veale poked me in the back and said, "Stop the lady-in-waiting!" Not knowing what to do, she had seen the man whom she was marching with going ahead, and she had ducked across and tried to get into the other line. I caught her by the fur coat and tried to pull her back. No luck. We went up and sat (out of order) in these benches and listened to a very formal address by the King, who made a good presentation. He was followed by the University Orator, who as usual had been compelled to write a formal address of tribute to both the King and Queen, in Latin. He read this, and we followed him from a printed sheet.

When the orator finished his address, we started to go down these steep steps. A man stood at the bottom, motioning left or right which person should come in order. He motioned to my side and I thought he was motioning to me; so I went ahead to where I thought I should have gone and so into the Royal Procession. We passed down to the entrance and went up through a long corridor, where I saw the University librarian. I was trying to get back to my proper spot, and as I gestured to him, he said, "Don't go back! Stay where you are." So I marched out into the courtyard in front of the new Bodleian, among the royal party, wearing my rented silk hat and morning coat.

The King reached the door and stuck the key in the lock, twisted it, and broke off the handle. The boys in the crowd began to laugh and some of them yelled a little. Ushers started to make a lane around to the back of the building, when some man with very strong fingers got hold of the shaft of the key and turned it. So we overcame that difficulty, and the procession broke up as we went into the building.

Now in that entryway they have the book with the names, engrossed on parchment, of all the people who gave large sums of money toward matching our money—I think it was four and a half million dollars—of which we gave sixty per cent. The book was opened to the page—when I saw it later—listing the Royal Society of Fishmongers, and lying on the book this broken key. There was a big trade fair in London at the time of the dedication. As the King broke the key, he is reported to have said, although it sounds like newspaper wisdom, "Britain can make it and Britain can break it." That was about the end of the ceremonial part. We had some very lovely social affairs, including dinners and teas, and all to the glory of the Foundation, I would say.

I ought to put in a word here about an occasion at Oxford, in 1948, when I was one of six Americans invited to come to the Congress of Chancellors of all the universities of the Commonwealth. It was a panorama picture of how British colonialism worked in the best years. These men came from all over the world. They were called to this meeting by the man in charge of the University Grants Commission. We sat in sessions for a whole week, and the first one, on new programs, was a very dramatic one for me, because you saw how their minds worked. As one man said, "We come here not to tell too many of our good ideas, but to get new ones."

The head of the University Grants Commission had a function similar to an officer of the Foundation; that is, he was head of the commission that made royal grants to all the universities and colleges in the Commonwealth. He opened the meeting with a long speech. Among other things, he brought up ideas on what they favored for each proposal. I think he made his mistake by saying where the money should go. This officer of the Treasury named not only the specific allotment for the next year, but the Oriental languages that he wanted strengthened. He also specified certain fields of study that he thought were not being properly cared for.

As he finished, one of the provincial rectors from Britain got up and answered, "Speaking for ourselves, it's a little hard to have anyone tell us what we should do." At lunch that day, he talked to me and said, "Do you think I was impudent?" I said, "No, I don't see where else you had a chance to protect yourselves." That afternoon, Oxford brought back its answer, which gave me a phrase I have never stopped using: Oxford respectfully declined the proposal and said it would "disturb the balance of studies." The commissioner, then — properly, I'm sure — felt rebuked. They wanted things in proportion. Everything should have its proper place in a pattern, and they didn't want the burden put on where it would not be properly carried. Incidentally, this meeting of the Commonwealth men gave me new ideas on things that we should do and could do for Oxford and Cambridge and all the other British institutions, such as Birmingham and Manchester.

GARD: Was this in conjunction with the opening of the Bodleian extension?

STEVENS: No, this had nothing to do with the Bodleian. This was in 1948, two years after the opening of the Bodleian extension, and it was related to the international educational programs of the British government.

II. Final Directions

GARD: David, the examples you have given of Foundation programs reflect the many successes of the Foundation in its various endeavors in the humanities and the arts; but in some cases, I'm sure, the outcome of a project was not a success. Could you relate for me some of the instances of the failures of your projects?

STEVENS: I don't know if I ever was refused anything by our loyal trustees and our presidents in the Humanities—the men that I've named—unless you want to include a couple of small things that Warren Weaver and I shared as our mutual loss through the intervention of a trustee, John Foster Dulles. Dulles was a pretty stiff, rock-ribbed man, who didn't say much. Warren Weaver and I both, at the end of the Second World War, wanted to revive things that we were deeply interested in. The *Scientific American* was on the rocks and needed public relations and some revival of subscriptions. And what I was interested in was at Oklahoma, a little journal called *Books Abroad,* at the University. It consisted of fine little reviews of new foreign books. Of course, it brought these books to Oklahoma for the editor to review. *Books Abroad* went all over the United States and abroad to let people know about new literary and historical works. We went in at the same meeting, just as the war ended, and asked for five thousand dollars for each of our proposals. I wanted to send sample copies of *Books Abroad* to Europe and renew subscriptions; and Warren wanted to publicize the value of the *Scientific American* and get a little start for their new program. Dulles, who was sort of a frosty son of a Presbyterian, said, "I don't think we'd better get into publication. Just drop them." They were afraid of publication, in a sense, as the General Education Board had not been, in that we subsidized a number of university presses heavily, as at the University of North Carolina, which in those years was turning out unusual social studies on the South. I think, perhaps, the trustees of a foundation are right not to get into the position of judging manuscripts. But if they want to help a journal, if they want to help a press, that's the important thing to do. Prompt help for publication of important manuscripts not of commercial appeal is basic to real philanthropy, but done indirectly.

GARD: Both *Scientific American* and *Books Abroad* are still in existence, I believe.

STEVENS: Yes. They both survived, and *Scientific American* is a great magazine, of course. *Books Abroad* is just what it always has been. The University of Oklahoma has free magazines, free books from all over the world, for review in *Books Abroad*. It covers several areas of the world, and readers go back to the publishers for books. It is a great idea which they have kept alive for fifty years.

One field where I'm sure we failed to capitalize on possibilities is in Ireland. I spent two weeks in Ireland on two visits toward the end of my service through the Foundation, and I was amazed at how ignorant I was of what a mass of important historical, literary, and linguistic work there is to do in Ireland right now. They have never had the money to do it. The National Folklore Commission, Trinity College, and all other institutional sources of programs in history are lively, but a lot of untouched raw material is buried in scores of boxes that a man by the name of Dr. James H. Delargy told me he had stored away in the warehouse of the National Folklore Commission. I think he had some hundred cases when I first discovered he was in need of help. He couldn't get them opened even to see what he had in them. He had scoured the country and had gathered them for solid study, but he lacked funds to undertake the work.

We could have spent fifty thousand dollars a year for ten years there, and had five good scholars at the end of that time who had learned all that was needed for their future careers while getting these manuscripts classified properly for the libraries. I don't know whether they have ever been catalogued. I doubt it.

GARD: How did you find out that this material existed?

STEVENS: Oh, by a visit of inquiry.

It was on this same trip, in 1949, that Chet D'Arms and I were in Wiesbaden, the headquarters of our Army, where he had a delightful stay. We were there to witness the return of many famous paintings that were rescued as our Army invaded. These paintings were then carried to the United States for security. I stood in front of a magnificent painting by Botticelli—in a crowded, made-over gallery where they had the ceremony of restoration. There were speeches of gratitude and all that, along with telling what the United States had done to save their paintings, their books, and their library materials.

GARD: One of the major problems in this country after the war was the wave of anti-communist feeling that affected the careers of many people. When we were talking about the Foundation's support of work in the Far East, you mentioned the political slander that worked against a man by the name of Owen Lattimore. This very possibly had an influence on what you did when you retired from the Rockefeller Foundation in 1950, in trying to make sure that, as much as you were able, the country was freed from the malign influence of such people as Joseph McCarthy, the Wisconsin senator.

STEVENS: Johnny Faulk's case is the best example. When he was a star broadcaster for CBS in radio and television, he was tainted by the criticism of so-called communism. I told that whole story to you, I think.

GARD: Not at all.

STEVENS: Johnny knew Frank Dobie when a graduate student in English, and Frank gave a thesis assignment relating to Negro folklore. Johnny knew all the leading black people. He got an admission to the funeral of a little boy and had his recording machine, not a tape recorder, out in the cornfield, next to the little church. He kept listening and watching his turntable. He became so emotionally worked up that he forgot to turn the disc and record the other side. He was a pioneer in gathering material on the Negro.

Johnny went on through that period, and when the war started, he couldn't make it into the Army because of a bad eye. So he went to work on a gasoline tanker from Texas to New York and wrote stories to amuse himself.

He turned up at our front door at Montclair once, in the middle of February during the war, and said, "Here I am—they let me off the boat. We were torpedoed just outside of New York harbor, and the boat is laid up in Hoboken for repairs. The captain said we could sleep on the boat if we wanted to, but there's no heat, no toilets, no food."

"So," he said, "I'm out here. What about my staying with you?" I said, "We're leaving tomorrow. Ruth's going with me on a trip down South for five weeks. You can have the house. But there is one thing. You mustn't go near the furnace. Old man Albie across the road runs the furnace, and if he finds anybody else fooling with it, he'll quit."

I wish you could have seen us when we came back and found Johnny having a good time taking care of things. "But," he said, "I've had some interesting times with Mr. Albie. He caught me down here poking the fire." You know, he was funny. There was nobody so funny as Johnny.

I know a lot about Johnny. He lost his job in Paterson because of this slander, and Louis Nizer, the great criminal lawyer, got interested in the case and spent a whole year getting ready for the trial. He sued this upstate chain grocer and two or three people besides for three and one-half million dollars. And he won his suit. Johnny didn't get anything out of it. He went back to Austin and tried to sell real estate.

Not long ago — I wish I had it to give you — a syndicated story of Johnny's appeared in the Los Angeles *Times*. He said, "Here's where I've taken to my *ark*. I can see what's coming. I bought a farm in west Texas and moved my wife and the children, and we're going to raise pigs and chickens and have a garden—and that's my ark—until the depression is over." He's a character.

GARD: Were there any problems with individuals the Foundation backed with grants?

STEVENS: You were supposed to find out if they were capable and if they had good credentials. One time we had two men who we thought were great, and later one of them was proved to be a communist. He got into trouble in Britain. He had to get out of the country. That's the only time we ever got tarred.

GARD: You had no idea this was going to happen?

STEVENS: I was led in. The man was supposed to know a lot about film production.

GARD: In other words, you would not have backed a grant to a communist?

STEVENS: No.

GARD: How was McCarthy undermining your work? Is there a connection?

STEVENS: No, I don't think so, except by attacks on such men as Owen Lattimore.

The day I left my office, I turned and looked back, and as I walked out the door, the painter was coming in to redecorate. And I thought, thank God, I'm through. Now I can do what I want to do. So I drove to Washington with Ruth to see a man whom we all knew as chairman of the Foreign Relations Committee, J. William Fulbright. I went to see him and said, "You have a great opportunity, I think, and much more to your credit than giving the fellowships called Fulbright Awards. Change the name. Give it up and call them the World Peace Awards." Well, he laughed and he said, "That's a nice idea." But he never did it.

GARD: Why did you approach Fulbright with your idea?

STEVENS: Because I thought it was a great opportunity to use a good title, "World Peace Awards," instead of making them a personal political plum. Make it international immediately.

Then I went on, and we had our first winter in California, and we came back. Ruth and I took a trip across Wisconsin and gathered opinions on Joe McCarthy. These were all very strong, adverse ones, which I used to build an article on him. It was published in a journal, *The Pacific Spectator*, that we had supported at Stanford University. It had been declined by two or three other journals as a little too hot for their good will. But *The Pacific Spectator* published this article on McCarthy.

III. Time and the Humanities

GARD: Did you ever get the feeling, working with the Foundation, that it was like a miniature government of people who went around the world doing good?

STEVENS: Well, I guess you could say that. There weren't many big foundations. Carnegie and ours were the only two good-sized ones, although there were a number of smaller ones. The Ford Foundation came later.

GARD: Did the stigma that was sometimes attached to the Rockefeller name ever become a problem for you?

STEVENS: Oh, no. I looked at it as Harper did. If someone would tell him that he shouldn't take that money, that it was "tainted money," Harper would say, "Give it to us, we'll fix it up."

GARD: How would you define the role of a foundation in contemporary life?

STEVENS: It has an objective purpose to help all of mankind, but it isn't the same as our American experience with foreign aid, where we have intended to help people by outright gifts. The foundation puts a man on the way to self-expression and self-support.

The head of the Prudential Life Insurance Company, Mr. Thomas I. Parkinson, was listening one day as I told of a term project that had been a success and was coming to an end. He stopped me at the end of my report to ask what became of the people. Who was taking care of them? I assured him that we were seeing that they were properly relodged in their old positions or in new ones, not just dropped cold after working on a project for several years.

The foundation purpose is always to contribute, not to sustain. It will help over a certain period, and then expects the person who is benefited to function on his own. As some older philanthropists in America have said, you ought, in each generation, to determine what can be done with philanthropy and to count on the next generation to expand in new directions where they find absolutely new needs. That explains in two ways, I think, the function of a foundation. Stimulate and let go.

CHARLES B. FAHS: The most important fact about Dave's leadership was that he had a broad and wise vision of what the humanities should be. This vision went far beyond his own background as a scholar in English literature. It was not restricted by the prevailing academic boundary lines and prejudices. His early, generous and crucial support for study of Asia, Russia, and the Arab world long before such studies were widely accepted in the scholarly community is a good example.

He was also a pioneer in supporting creative work in theatre and writing in the universities and even in extension programs. He did not hesitate to support creative work outside the university environment as well and thus paved the way for the later arts program of the Rockefeller Foundation. Within the budget limits available to him he sought to give the humanities new meaning, content, and vitality.

EDWARD F. D'ARMS: Dave is, and was, essentially a quiet person. He never dominated a group by out-talking others, but the alert way in which he followed the speakers, one after the other, and the brief, crisp questions he interposed from time to time left no doubt who was in command.

His decisions were arrived at quietly, too. Rarely did he give a detailed account of the arguments pro and con, or a summary of the varying views, and yet it was clear that he had weighed them all.

In my ten years at the Rockefeller Foundation (almost eight of them after Dave had retired), the most frequent opening of a conversation with a potential grantee was, "How's Dave Stevens? He's a wonderful person. He helped me greatly at a time when I needed help." And this help was not always a grant; often it was advice or a sympathetic ear.

GARD: Let's turn to the function of the humanities. How are we going to define that term?

STEVENS: You are talking about a term that has so many facets you don't need to worry about defining the whole except to say that it relates to every contact of humanity with the past and with the present and the individual's appreciation and expression of it all. These disciplines, particularly history, literature, philosophy, and language, as well as the expressive arts, are the outlets. Here are some definitions which show the real unity of mankind. They are what make mankind civilized instead of barbarous.

GARD: Looking back over your many years as director for the Humanities, how do you view the changes that have taken place in the humanities?

STEVENS: I can easily see that some of the changes that have occurred since 1930 make the present look very, very different in perspective. Archeology has become much more of a gradual professional operation, but it is threatened somewhat by the crudescence of anthropology. That subject makes young people think that they are doing something great and novel if they follow Margaret Mead's line of language on the social side, or the line that is common here in a university such as Lawrence, which sends students out to do field work in places where it is known there were Indian cultures. That's very enjoyable, lots of fun, but I'm not sure if it's worthwhile. In contrast, solid archeology, which is going on now as we know in Asia Minor, where they have recently turned up important objects; in China; and in Israel—those things are fundamental and persist. But I hope that anthropology does not waste the time of young people who ought to be spending their learning period on substance, in history, in cultural backgrounds, in language, or in matters that have something to do with the real learning value of the humanities.

I think America is on the edge of a very unusual growth. I think we are out of the compulsion of the period of novelty in art. Dance has become an American form. Right now it has several centers in the major cities of America. Now it is more than ever a teaching subject in institutions. The same thing may be said of orchestras. The big symphonies that have developed in the last fifteen or twenty years are now being supported by Federal money. Although these symphonies never will be self-supporting, the people in communities are beginning to accomplish what Cleveland did as long as forty years ago, taking the orchestras to themselves and making them part of the local culture. We can list many of them that have been in this style for a good many years, and others that I'm sure I don't know anything about, in symphonic and chamber music, have developed in many cases in connection with universities.

I would say that the study of foreign languages has now become a part of the area studies that grew out of the war. Now students can gain something beyond reading and speaking a language. They learn something about the foreign world. There are study centers abroad across Europe, many in the Far East, and students take foreign language as a start toward these seminars. Two-thirds of the centers I know of are really creative and lead to a totally new world outlook for our students.

So instead of fighting against the language departments, many college and university students are going back to them. In some universities and colleges Latin and Greek have even come back very strongly into the curriculum. Students are going back to these classical languages as essential for a humanistic perspective.

GARD: Why is it that when the five Foundation divisions are mentioned, humanities is listed last?

STEVENS: Oh, that's because it's the least appealing to human nature. Why do they start with public health? Because people care more for their selfish guts and they want to be helped or protected, physically. Or, we have an epidemic of hookworm in the South and we can't take care of it. Or foot-and-mouth disease in Mexico, where the Foundation spent nine million dollars to eradicate it.

When I went to Greece, the King told me, "Give us dams and reforestation. We'll pay for all these things." Well, that wasn't my job. I was out there to put in a museum in the Agora, right in the center of Athens. Of course, you have to get your economic base to grow. But meanwhile, all the big strong countries who have a seasoned culture have a great responsibility to maintain it and to spread it.

GARD: How would you describe the process of educating a humanist?

STEVENS: First of all, you start with the simple task of teaching children to use their own language and later giving them a background in foreign languages. Then, before they get out of preparatory school, they ought to have the rudiments of philosophy, ethics, logic, aesthetics, and their relation to life, literature, and religion. With this also they need to have a mythological, religious, and spiritual background to go with the classics and the *Bible*. If they don't have that by the end of preparatory school, they are not apt to be humanistic by nature.

Of course, reading and writing are the two great tools. If we don't give them to the average student, he will not have the verbal force with which to attack his studies. You have your learning period and your creative or expressive, or teaching period. I don't think you get a good humanist, as a teacher, as quickly as you get a good teacher of science; he teaches the fundamental laws, while there are fewer laws in our field than in any other. A man is a law to himself.

GARD: What are the laws in our field?

STEVENS: Intense interest in subject matter and the ability to deal with people and emotions, with history and philosophy, and the substance of what you mean by the human race. You must get your vocabulary and your sense of values; then you have a personality. It starts in childhood.

Nothing but the humanities rests so heavily on growth through time. You rarely get a great humanist till he's forty. You need to build up such a background of knowledge.

In the end, the humanities, which have always pervaded life, and every kind of human being, relate to what values in the past apply today and will tomorrow. The humanist gives man his faith in the future, his message of hope, and the relationship of philosophy and religion to all of his aspirations. You start with scholarship, to maintain and increase your sense of values; to protect them you work through the individual who can apply the values of the humanities in order to make a contribution through his own work, or through what his children do, or what society does.

Part Three
What Are the Humanities?

by
David Stevens

For Ruth

The humanities are not useful, but they are necessary. They are essential to the good life even of the humblest people, who may be too poor in any sense to cultivate them, for the fate of these people will not be pleasant if their masters, however just, are not humane.

George Sarton

This question, "What are the humanities?" is met today by each person at the level of his emotional and intellectual experience. One who has had little concern with the backgrounds of these main streams of life may think this word to be equivalent to "human"—which it is not. In general, the public mind attaches the term to recalled hours in the more formal kind of entertainment—at dramatic or musical performances, for example—and associates them with the names of actors, playwrights, and composers. Those who know the term in its academic setting have a general idea that humanities are different from sciences and social studies. Among these the more reflective college graduates will recall certain courses, the teachers who gave them insights into literary and artistic values, or the personal satisfaction that was gained from active experience in any of the arts, such as music, dance, or dramatic performance.

The humanities are all these inward and outward signs of emotional, intellectual satisfaction. They are the forms in which we create a social relationship. At their source, they are the stream of experiences and beliefs that mankind passes on into the hearts and minds of men. However the individual defines the humanities, he is in debt to scholars and interpreters and to all that scholars and interpreters have made vital for the living generation. The individual is inheritor, if he has power to use it so, of all that these two classes of men have given him.

The source of old and new knowledge in our time are the universities, because they enable the individual to discover and interpret new ideas and experiences. They, too, are among the lasting institutions to keep safe what is known and to inculcate that in the lives of men. In universities the term "humanities" has as precise a designation as the term "sciences." Throughout graduate schools each has many branches of specialization. The subdivisions of humanities are set within such broad terms as language, literature, history, philosophy; of the sciences, mathematics, physics, chemistry, and biology. The social sciences have less clearly marked primary headings, perhaps, but the direction of effort is as sharply defined for the beginning of real research.

The humanities have their roots in all languages, all literatures, all histories, and in all philosophical-religious experiences. Critical writings on individuals or their work or on the environments within which they worked, and all representations of human thought and feeling, whether real or imagined, qualify within the most ample definition of the humanities. Such qualities must be kept alive in the present and for the future by the academic humanist. Magnificent examples outside the academic world appear, as will be shown by example, but the roots and main branches of humanistic growth are within the graduate schools of universities.

The familiar words of Matthew Arnold give us the duty of the humanist in our time, "to learn and propagate the best that is known and thought in the world." A definition of the humanities for today is in the remarkable book by Howard Mumford Jones, *One Great Society: Humane Learning in the United States.** His title for the work of a committee of the American Council of Learned Societies is from lines in Wordsworth's *Prelude:*

> There is
> One great society alone on earth;
> The noble Living and the noble Dead.

In that society are the humanists. For a lifetime each has devoted himself to a particular purpose—to discover, recall, interpret, and pass on the meanings of life in person and through the work of his students, who will carry on the great tradition. Jones himself is a superb example of such care. The twelve chapters of his book state the place of the humanist in society.

A hundred years were needed to advance the humanities in this country to their present state. A short review of origins properly introduces definitions and examples. For beginnings Americans looked to Germany for fields of study and research as well as for methods. When The Johns Hopkins University opened in 1876, German patterns for work in the humanities had authority, as in certain professional fields. Its president, Daniel Coit Gilman, readily applied what he had gathered during his two

---

*(New York: Harcourt, Brace and Company, Inc., 1959)

years abroad with his friend Andrew D. White, his comrade as an undergraduate in Yale University. Gilman began his studies at Norwich Academy, in Connecticut, took his degree at Yale University in 1852, and spent one year at Harvard University before crossing to Europe for study and travel. For the following seventeen years he participated in the work of the Sheffield Scientific School, in New Haven, as an administrator, teacher, and librarian. These experiences strengthened his powers for the years of his presidency of the University of California and for his great work as first president of The Johns Hopkins University.

Gilman set the pattern for the University. It was to have a small undergraduate school and a strong graduate one that would be its main body dedicated to research as to teaching. The perspective in his mind appears in the allocations within that first budget: one-fourth was allotted to the library and three-fourths to salaries of forty-four members of its faculty. The faculty had been assembled from several foreign countries and from other American institutions. For the humanities, the most notable appointment was Basil L. Gildersleeve, in Greek, from the University of Virginia. The cost of buildings and their maintenance was made incidental to full care of a limited faculty and their library. This was a landmark in educational history in this country, and it was followed by others with a similar purpose.

This emphasis on graduate work was followed with plans for Clark University in Massachusetts, under the leadership of G. Stanley Hall. His selection of faculty was so admirable that shortly he found many of his men being carried away by William Rainey Harper for the new University of Chicago. The emphasis there for the future was demonstrated in the fact that when the University of Chicago opened, two-thirds of its students were enrolled for graduate studies—a ratio that is there today.

Two of these three university presidents were deeply involved in humanities personally. Gilman had made his commitment to the library as a fundamental resource, next to faculty choices, for the future. At the University of Chicago Harper continued his work in Hebrew, first as teacher along with his administrative duties, then on a national scale through home correspondence. He aroused the entire world of scholarship by the establishment of scholarly journals, at times promising men under invitation to the Chicago faculty to create one for the general reader and a second for strictly research materials. To a degree Gilman followed his example. In order to benefit his own faculty and to open the way for others, Harper created his University Press, today one of the leaders among the large number of presses widening the range of American sciences and the humanities.

Building great collections for the libraries of public and private institutions to compare with those in the older universities of the eastern states has taxed the ingenuity and the resources of newer universities; yet the evenness of supply to scholars has greatly improved under changes in distribution through loans and copying. At the center of this present system, which brings needed materials from all the world to the desk of any serious scholar, is the Library of Congress. It would be a waste of type to list the major gains given the humanities by its service to the individual scholar. Two are its distribution abroad, free of charge, of runs of journals contributed by American scholars, and its buying program to bring for deposit in designated American libraries useful new printed matter from as many foreign countries. One example illustrates the power of the Library of Congress to make this the foremost country for scholarship. Some years ago a French scholar was to start his exhaustive research on Shakespeare. He quickly decided that time and money would be saved by doing all his work in the United States at the Folger Library and the Library of Congress.

Today the definition of Emerson matches that of Matthew Arnold on the function of scholars, to disseminate "the best that has been thought and known in the world." Emerson wrote that it is "the function of the scholar to cheer, to raise, and to guide men by showing them facts amid appearances." Also, he asked later, in his Phi Beta Kappa address in 1837, for a new intellectual sweep in this country through philosophy and the arts. Emerson was calling for the same spirit of self-reliance that in the Middle Ages broke the intellectual and spiritual bondage of humanity.

My own commentary on the responsibility of the scholar to his own generation and the future is in *The Changing Humanities*, published in 1953. One passage reads as follows:

Today, with a world-wide opportunity for the increase of cultural and personal contacts among men, they [the humanities] have new, universal responsibilities. The narrower channels of humane studies today have been widened to carry the full flow of fact and meaning at full tide and are waiting to be filled.

The great traditions of learning are not exclusive possessions of scholars. They never have been, any more than are the ways of expression in the arts. In our time both learning and the arts have come to greater influence in the day-by-day life of the people. This is true in spite of mechanized amusement and political misuse of the arts and artists by dictators. Denial of freedom of thought, by either expedient, has not stopped men from creative effort and self-expression in any but the captive countries. Such sweeping denials of human rights as do exist today will not in the end overcome the rights of citizens to learn and of artists to create. Meanwhile, promise of finer and fuller development through the arts is fore-shadowed by the strength of the humanistic disciplines in this country and by the lively attention of the American public to all new ideas in education.

For their part, the humanists in and out of universities have two obligations—to increase the body of learning and to interpret human values for the benefit of the public mind. When they do both, they are at their full task. They will not want for followers so long as they demonstrate in practice the interplay of research, teaching and interpretation dealing with the personal values in life.

Perpetually the humanities, as disciplines to maintain knowledge of the part of man in his universe, face a single question that bears on every individual act and judgment. . . .

. . . Though employing methods that in part are those of the sciences and the social sciences, with respect to function they are unique: by interpreting a galaxy of human acts and aspirations, the effect upon individuals of all types of experience throughout recorded time, and the concern of Man with God and Nature, they reveal the range of individual choices in all environments. Their function is not to discover so much as to show the ways to self-discovery.*

More striking because coming from a humanist of high place in all generations, are the words of Eduard Schwartz, who left this passage to be read at his funeral as a profession of faith:

In the prime of life I addressed these words to a learned gathering: "The world cannot endure without compromises, but scholarship [Wissenschaft] goes to ruin if it does not work out problems sharply and if it consents to bargain away somewhat of their antitheses. Scholarship does not, like the preacher, bring peace, nor does it unfetter hearts, as the poets do; but the few who take upon themselves the yoke of enquiry are concerned that life and movement may remain in the spirit of humanity, and that the endless striving and endless yearning after knowledge may not fall asleep. That is not everything, but yet it is so much that those few must not complain if they give for it a life full of doubt and restlessness, full of abnegation and loneliness." I used the same words in writing to the Theological Faculty of Strassburg when they gave me an honorary doctorate in 1917 on the occasion of their Luther celebration. Now too, at the close of my life, I take back nothing of them, but only add, my soul belongs to Almighty God: His will be done.**

---

*The Changing Humanities: An Appraisal of Old Values and New Uses (New York: Harper & Brothers, 1953), pp. xi-xii.
**Stevens, p. 232.

This translation by Arthur D. Nock is a kind of testament for all scholars, more durable than stone and more animate than mere words. Both writer and translator possessed something unknown to those who are untouched by the light of scholarly insights. All who heard or have read this translation by Nock, used in his address before the Harvard Divinity School in 1949, remember it. His words prove the power of inspired translation so that meanings are fixed in memory at first hearing.

In this address Nock stated the case for religious teaching and study in a passage that concluded with the sentence, "The serious study of religion is a part of humanistic study in general, and for its well-being needs to be conducted in a community where history, language, and philosophy receive the full service of scholars who have integrity, competence, and zeal." These last words brought a comment from Edward H. Levi while still president of the University of Chicago: "I do wish you might say more about religion or theology. At a conference at Notre Dame of seven divinity school deans, a few university presidents . . . and some foundation people, I was asked whether divinity students were of any importance to the universities — and the assumption was that they were not. I guess I shocked and perhaps pleased some people by saying that I could not imagine the University of Chicago without the study of religion or theology, and I regarded them as integral to the humanities."

These statements of three educators, far apart in time and in chief interests, stress the place of the university in society and the part of religion in both learning and living. Eduard Schwartz testified to need of the humanities and of dedicated scholars for their perpetual growth. Arthur D. Nock and Edward H. Levi made religious values "integral to the humanities." They represented the practices of two leading universities in making religion a subject for instruction and for constant investigation. Nothing less than this would preserve the balance of studies to give a right basis for human conduct.

This balance of studies within the humanities gives all other disciplines the elements necessary for their perpetuation within the framework of a living, creative society. Drawing upon all that man has created, and now creates, as the enduring record of human learning and experience, the humanities contribute to the individual development of all people in three ways—the intellectual, the aesthetic, and the spiritual.

What becomes of a society when these sources of civilized thought and behavior are forgotten? What is the consequence for future generations when a society lapses into animalism? A clear and final answer to both questions is in the homely saying of a Georgia circuit rider. Talking with Ellis Gibbs Arnall, governor of his state during the forties, he said, "You know what I think? I think that everything that you do, or I do, affects not only what is going to happen but what already has happened, years and centuries ago. Maybe you can't change what has passed, but you can change all the meaning of what has passed. You can even take all the meaning away."* These words tell all that one needs to know about the dangers of dictatorship and also of the values in historical perspective, through knowledge, to prevent those dangers. All who give increase in such knowledge and disseminate it are the guarantors of intellectual freedom. They guard against the attacks of ignorant or willful men, for it is through knowing truth that people learn that ideals are weapons, and that they are to be found only in a free society.

There are many Americas in the one. In certain matters all should be in harmony. At the opening of the University of Chicago, President Harper said, "The question before us is how to become one in spirit, not necessarily in opinion." This signifies that we are to have common cultural values of the sort that literature, history, and the arts bring. When a person has them from an early age, he develops the common interests on which later and constantly he will develop personal ones. The principle is established in the individual and in a society that is "one in spirit" wherever the humanities exist. In contrast are those persons and those societies without values created by intellectual and ethical forces. An example of this is the bleakness of spectator sports, before a television screen or on a bench of a sports arena or in an outdoor park. Such diversions add nothing to personality or to self-expression, as do the humanities in a myriad of ways.

What thus far has been shown of the power in humanities to develop character, intellect, and vision likewise tells how the driving purposes of dedicated scholars create the body of new and usable knowledge on which the humanities exist and grow. A great teacher can illustrate moderately the meaning of this dedication, by disseminating knowledge or by giving the ability of creative self-expression to others. The following examples show how within a lifetime a humanist can make a lasting impression upon future life in his own society and even around the world for an indeterminate time.

For example, Helen Waddell (1889-1945) brought into universal appreciation and enjoyment a new era in cultural history. She gathered up the verse of the Middle Ages, translated it out of the Latin of that period, and interpreted its secular and religious meanings. She brought the meanings and symbols of medieval Latin into easy reach of any trained mind and placed them in common languages of today. Also she inspired others to work in the original materials. Her masterpiece, *The Wandering*

---

*Walter R. Agard, *et al.*, *The Humanities for Our Time* (Lawrence, Kan.: Univ. of Kansas Press, 1949), p. 27.

Scholars, came to print in 1927 and met with such acceptance that three more printings followed within two years. Her one field of intense study yielded a clear view of the Latin lyric out of texts written in the difficult Latin of the Middle Ages.

Throughout the twelfth century and on into the fifteenth century western Europe used Latin as the medium of communication for all but the most casual purposes. Miss Waddell wrote in her Introduction, "It was not only the language of literature, of the Church, of the law-courts, of all educated men, but of ordinary correspondence."* Out of this utilitarian use came the secular songs and lyrics brought to understanding through this book. What she began as a preface to her translations became a sweeping review of all in the life of the people through the words of wandering scholars and minstrels. She opened to readers the inmost thought and feeling of a long period, which became a source of understanding and enjoyment.

A consequence was to turn humanists toward a new source of reading and interpretation. Only four years after the first printing of *The Wandering Scholars* in 1927, Philip Schuyler Allen of the University of Chicago brought out his own book, *Medieval Latin Lyrics,* in which constant use of Miss Waddell's translations and interpretations demonstrated her influence as a result of lifelong work in a new field of scholarship.

The potentials for this effort by Helen Waddell were in both her heredity and environment. Her tenacity of purpose was the third factor for success. She was born in Tokyo of missionary parents. Their scholarly bent made her turn naturally toward scholarship, while her contacts from childhood made Chinese and Japanese next to her native tongue in daily use. She wrote and spoke both languages easily. When she was sent back to the homeland of her parents for education, she took a degree at the University of Belfast. She went on to study and to teach at Oxford University, living in Somerville College and Lady Margaret's Hall, with absences on the Continent for periods of study in France and Italy. Her standing in scholarship is defined by the award of an honorary degree by Columbia University and election to an honorary membership in the Medieval Academy of America. The proof of the value of her life of work in one cultural field can be seen in the effect on the individual who reads her book. He finds his imagination aroused, his understanding brightened, and his spirit lifted to a new level. He realizes that he is having a totally new experience.

The Introduction of *The Wandering Scholars* tells in its first lines what is in store:

----

*(Boston: Houghton, Mifflin Co., 1927), p. x.

There is no beginning, this side the classics, to a history of mediaeval Latin; its roots take hold too firmly on the kingdoms of the dead. The scholar's lyric of the twelfth century seems as new a miracle as the first crocus; but its earth is the leafdrift of centuries of forgotten scholarship. His emotional background is of his own time; his literary background is pagan, and such furniture as his mind contains is classical or pseudo-classical . . . . To the mediaeval scholar, with no sense of perspective, but a strong sense of continuity, Virgil and Cicero are but upper reaches of the river that still flows past his door. The language in which they wrote is still the medium of the artist, even the creative artist: it was so, even in the seventeenth century, to Milton, still more to Bacon.*

Other lines give a sense of the transition from classical originals to the pseudo-classical forms of the Middle Ages:

Dido, Queen of Carthage, was the romantic heroine of the Middle Ages. They could not read the lines of Homer where the old men on the wall hushed their swallows' chattering as Helen passed by; they knew her only in Dictys — sweet-natured, long-limbed and golden-haired, or in the amazing flashlight vision of Virgil, crouching on the steps of the Temple of Vesta in the light of the fires, 'Erynnis to her father's house and Troy.' She is Absolute Beauty, even as *Venus generosa*.**

When Helen Waddell brought the spirit and life of the Middle Ages into free use of all later generations by her translations and interpretations of Latin lyrics, she gave proof of the everlasting need for the scholar who can reveal a hidden part of the human story to the public mind. Such work ranks with the results from an important archeological discovery or new meanings brought from a long-hidden manuscript.

At the end of scholarship based on close, difficult translation and interpretation of small bodies of evidence came Helen Waddell's book to show the scholar's lyric of the twelfth century "as new a miracle as the first crocus; but its earth is the leafdrift of centuries of forgotten scholarship."

At the opposite end in scholarly research is finished interpretation of masses of evidence to winnow out a lasting part of human culture, such as *The Decline and Fall of the Roman Empire* by Edward Gibbon. In contrast to the masterpiece of Helen Waddell, that of Edward Gibbon has had far greater influence on readers, including those in all literate countries.

---

*Waddell, p. ix.
**Waddell, p. xxiii.

Gibbon lived from 1737 to 1794. His formal studies in the university were slight. It was constant income from his father that made it possible for him to travel and study without interruption for his lifetime. The appeal of the subject began when, at the age of fourteen, he read Echard's *Roman History*. His resolve to work on the history of Rome came in 1764, under dramatic circumstances. Gibbon wrote that "musing amid the ruins of the Capitol, where the barefooted boys were singing vespers in the temple of Jupiter, the idea of writing the decline and fall of the city first started in my mind." Twenty-three years later, on June 27, 1787, he wrote the last word. He had created the most definitive work of history in the English language, in the judgment of Sir Leslie Stephen. It soon was translated into eleven foreign languages and is steadily reprinted. The standard edition in English, that of John Bury, has been out since 1900; for students and the general reader, fresh printings issue regularly from the Oxford University Press.

Unusual facts surround the appearance of the successive volumes of the first edition. The painstaking care in its preparation is shown by Gibbon's statement that the first and last volumes were wholly rewritten three times. Volume one was out in 1776. Volumes two and three were out five years later, in 1781. Then it was that the Duke of Gloucester made his unlettered comment, "Another damned thick book! Always scribble, scribble, scribble — eh, Mr. Gibbon?" The work went on. Six years later the task was done. Through nearly two centuries, in spite of change by important additions to knowledge through constant scholarly investigation, *The Decline and Fall of the Roman Empire* remains a standard title. As extraordinary is the fact that it was created by one scholar when library resources were few and widely scattered, and the traditional patronage of authors at its close.

A third example of results from scholarship has the merit of work by individuals like Helen Waddell and Edward Gibbon, and also the immediate service to a national need that came from demands of war. As an inheritor of a sense of scholarship through family background, this American scholar demonstrated the practical possibilities of action in many fields. John Matthews Manly (1865-1940), of a distinguished southern family, was son of the president of a university and grandson of the president of another. His education in school and college had its center in mathematics, which he taught for a few years before entering Harvard University. The granting of his degree in philology was the first Ph.D. given in this subject and prefaced a year of steady reading covering many fields of knowledge. These five years at Harvard led to appointment in 1891 to a professorship in Brown University. He remained there until 1898, when he left to head the Department of English Language and Literature at Harper's University of Chicago. He remained there until retirement in 1933.

There he created a program in undergraduate and graduate studies for unbroken coverage during a four-quarter year. It required a large staff and much use of visiting faculty for teaching and carrying on work toward the master's and doctor's degrees. He taught his seminar in Chaucer and his Methods of Research, as well as one in medieval drama. Manly broadened the scope of teaching and research in English language and literature, and also made a place in graduate studies for work in literary criticism and original composition. Under his associates in the department new writers of prose and poetry were developed whose writings became significant nationally and for readers in all English-speaking countries. The Chicago magazine *Poetry* had its first issue on September 23, 1912, with members of the University faculty in English among its sponsors and with the student body its patrons. One of the students later became its editor. Contributions came from the whole world of British and American poets. Its circulation was and still is international.

Manly's chief studies were devoted to Chaucer and to *Piers Plowman*. Under his scrutiny this poem, traditionally accepted as by a single author, became on the basis of the evidence of style and its substance, the work of three men. Two works on Chaucer in very different degrees of significance were his book *Some New Light on Chaucer* (1926) and the eight volumes of *The Canterbury Tales* (1940). The first gave his identifications of contemporary figures in the several pilgrims named in the *Prolog*; the second, from an examination of every line in some eighty known manuscripts, identified finally a true text. This monumental work by Manly and his colleague Edith Rickert came from the University of Chicago Press only a few months before his death in the spring of 1940. The ten years of word-by-word analysis and comparisons produced, as close to the poet's original text as is possible, what Chaucer actually wrote; the thousands of variant readings made by successive scribes were eliminated. The eight volumes include all this evidence and discussion of the methods used to obtain and to produce a definitive text.

His public service came during the First World War, when he developed for the Army a bureau for analysis of cipher and code messages. This called for the training of nearly three hundred men, among whom were five of his departmental staff in the University.

For scholars his contribution came out of his presidency of the Modern Language Association. Manly made the annual meetings productive by changing from a sequence of addresses by older members to a reading of papers and discussion of them by those in special groups. Each has its own chairman to direct the meeting of twenty to fifty specialists in a chosen field. Selected papers are discussed intensively by participants whose criticisms may be the qualifying cause for publication of a paper in the journal of the Association. The democratic process stimulates attendance at annual meetings and a spirit of vitality in the research and teaching of literature, language, and literary history.

Professor Manly also had concern for the constant improvement of teaching in preparatory school and in colleges. Through the study of English a pupil determines his future success in any subject, to a degree, and there he develops all his basic interest in the humanities as a part of life. Manly therefore brought into the classroom and to private study the first books of selections from English prose and poetry, giving on a historical basis an orderly presentation of literary values. His book *English Poetry* appeared in 1907 and his *English Prose* in 1909. In 1916 the two came out as a single volume, with translations of older pieces in Anglo-Saxon as well as contemporary pieces. This third issue had 750 pages of text and thirty pages of notes. Every volume had the same prefatory note: "This book has been made in response to the wishes of teachers who need a collection in a single volume with notes."

With the same purpose to help all advanced courses in British and American literatures and also the individual reader, Manly brought out two other books. His *Contemporary English Literature* was ready for use in 1921, and was revised in 1928 and 1935. His *Contemporary American Literature* was out in 1922, with revisions in 1929 and 1934. They contain biographical data on each author, lists of critical articles on them, and titles of their works. This sequence of volumes was the work of Manly and his two colleagues, Edith Rickert and Fred B. Millett.

Many other scholars made similar contributions to the American tradition in English studies, by changing methods of teaching and research. This is true as well for other disciplines in the humanities. Historical studies covering the American westward movement began in 1885 under Frederick Jackson Turner and more intensive cultivation of studies on Latin America in 1911 under Herbert Eugene Bolton. Carl Lotus Becker had many new views that influenced the history of economics and politics, but his greatest interest was in the history of ideas. In the second quarter of this century the scientific study of linguistics had its beginnings under Leonard Bloomfield and Edward Sapir, opening the field of dialect studies, which is now significant for social and economic research. The trend toward cultural history, with social and literary consequences, had important influences on new work in the humanities following the publication in 1930 of Vernon Parrington's three-volume *Main Currents in American Thought*. The influence on scholarship was evident from these new directions of work.

Also, graduate studies in the humanities were changing as early as 1910. The English faculty of Harvard University had liberalized the terms governing subject matter by opening the way for research toward higher degrees by new paths. Choices of subjects for doctoral theses were permitted beyond the period of the English Renaissance, and linguistics began to displace the term "philology." Comparative literature became a research form. Scholarly inquiry into early periods of American literature became part of the increased interest in other aspects of national culture. Graduate students had credits toward higher degrees from Bliss Perry's stimulating course on prose fiction, which was a favorite among undergraduates; the same access to the undergraduate course in Shakespeare, under George Lyman Kittredge, gave graduate students a demonstration of a teaching method which they could accept or not for their future careers. The fundamentals of British drama were systematically revealed in the year course under George Pierce Baker, where a mingling of undergraduates brought them into appreciation of the need in all teaching to make critical judgments a part of the study of sources and literary tradition. Baker also admitted the qualified graduate student to his course English 47, for original work in playwriting. This access was matched by the chance to be in the course in writing under Le Baron Russell Briggs.

An important member of the faculty in English was William Allan Neilson. The end of a lecture by Neilson led to a gathering of students around him in the hallway near his door, in order to ask questions on critical methods that were stimulated by his lectures and writings. In 1906 Neilson had published his edition of Shakespeare's plays, following his research work on the early quartos and the First Folio. Five years later, in 1911, came his *Chief Elizabethan Dramatists*. In 1912 appeared the title that had most effect on criticism and interpretation, his *Essentials in Poetry,* which carried his meanings across the country as they had once held his students after the end of a lecture to talk at the door of his lecture room.

Other gains for scholarship and teaching came from the mind and spirit of John Livingston Lowes (1887-1945). After study in Leipzig and Berlin he entered Harvard University and received his doctor's degree in 1905. He demonstrated in his research and in his teaching the qualities that brought him back in 1918 to the English faculty at Harvard. The next year he published his *Convention and Revolt in Poetry* to express his methods of criticism. Through reading in Coleridge's Notebooks, he centered his research upon the processes of creative writing based on ideas and images gathered from many sources. The outcome was the publication in 1927 of his *Road to Xanadu.* The processes of critical analysis and synthesis in Lowes' book were called by Neilson "a most triumphant demonstration of the type of scholarship of which he is the most distinguished and most highly recognized exponent in America."

Among the graduate students under the guidance of Lowes was Douglas Bush, who later said, "I had the happy experience of writing my Ph.D. thesis under Lowes." Much later, when he was a member of the department and had made important contributions to the Milton record, he wrote, "When I began, research was the established ideal; but I have come to believe that in the present state of our own civilization, at home as well as in the world at large, the chief need is to keep the humanities alive and to help enlarge the saving remnant who find strength and light in great literature."

These statements give the full definition of the function of the humanities. When a scholar of first rank says that "the end of learning is life," not "the end of life is learning," he brings these two aims of service into balance. Researcher and interpreter are at their respective tasks for the public good. The final estimate given by Bush puts the burden of the humanist at the present time on the side of the interpreter.

The three examples I have given to illustrate the ways of life for the scholar also express the necessity for that total and lifelong devotion to a purpose on the part of the scholar, and demonstrate the radiating effects from scholarly accomplishment into all social and educational values. Helen Waddell gave herself completely to the translation and interpretation of the poetry from a generation of wandering scholars. Edward Gibbon worked with masses of evidence in order to winnow out his conclusions on the causes of the loss of a world empire. The third, John Manly, assisted a long line of research scholars to become interpreters and critics of literature and history. Through his own studies and the application of a wide knowledge in all aspects of literature and language, he served the full requirements put upon the humanist. He brought a great increase in understanding to his own generation and to those in the future.

Then, too, there are the services of those scholars who keep current some absolutely essential tool of human life and thought. Among these are the commonplace task, as it seems to the uninitiated, of making dictionaries and other works of reference. Since Samuel Johnson finished the first English dictionary for public use, single-handedly, without benefit of patronage, the trade has seen steady progress in making dictionaries. The most familiar examples are those with definitions in the language of the words defined, and the book made for definitions of a foreign language that has the words in the language of the used. These works are the conservers of knowledge as well as servers of the public mind within their own generation.

In simplest form the writing and speech of any individual come from use. All five senses are involved in gaining a vocabulary. George Herbert Palmer gave the directions for this increase in personal vocabulary. At any age a person can add words to his vocabulary by the simple process of using them. Once used, a word and so its idea or meanings become a part of personal word stock. Palmer added that it is mere laziness that keeps anyone confined within a meager vocabulary. What was true in his day is still more true today, when careful use of words is much less the case than in his time. Speech then was effective from the lecture platform, and writing was more common in the total population, within educational requirements of schools, exchange of ideas by letters, wide reading, and conversation. In his time there were more family magazines, few spectator sports, no radio or television, and no films. Time spent in reading books was considerable at all age levels.

In his years at Harvard University a first-year undergraduate wrote a daily theme of a few pages and deposited it as directed. This exercise in self-discipline brought completed sentences and paragraphs to paper, and a knowledge of idiomatic forms and meanings of words. Today, in contrast, formal training in English composition as a first-year college requirement in this country is uncommon, and secondary schools no longer send up to colleges the disciplined students needing only such proof of ability as was given by the daily theme routine. Practices in secondary schools often center in use of workbooks that ask for choice of the word among four printed under a sentence for insertion in the blank space. There is no exercise in structure of sentence or paragraph. Mechanical checking of a page in a workbook sets the score for the lesson, the workbook is finally destroyed, and the student may or may not have been required to demonstrate his knowledge of composition or to create a coherent text. Such practices do not lead toward a wide gathering of new words or to the silent reading that carries one into an unfamiliar environment. People and places in all time, past and present, as well as those which exist beyond reality within the mind of an author, can be found within the covers of a book.

The word "book" brings to mind the useful and frustrating influences upon the reader by the book trade. The steady flow of paperbacks from all manner of outlet, such as direct mail, or the racked copies in supermarkets and elsewhere, which are determined by shrewd judges of public demand, has a tremendous force. For the common reader this is the elemental form of book reviewing, done through the sales appeal of a bright-colored cover. New hard-cover books have review in newspapers, weekly and monthly magazines, and by listings weekly so long as they are among the best ten in sales. These are valid guides, to a degree, for new titles. The book clubs, which enlist members under terms of annual acceptances from recommendations to their nationwide clientele, stimulate and guide readers; but they also have added restrictions on personal judgment by their power of choice and the fact that delivery is made unless promptly cancelled by a subscriber. Two positive sources of choice are the credible reviews in the printed media or, for old and young alike, the recommendation of trained librarians.

The American library is the alternative for comprehensive bookstores, which do not exist except in large centers of population. It is the source of advice and of supply in even small towns across the country. Old books are there or can be had on loan through orders from the librarian. New titles are added under discriminating selection of personnel who are trained to be objective critics of value.

Two admonitions of Ruskin are effective for personal judgments. One is the familiar warning that if you do *this* you cannot do *that*. The other is his warning, "Life being very short, and the quiet hours of it few, we ought to waste none of them in reading worthless books." In his day the writer had easier relations with publishers and new titles were far fewer than today.

Perhaps this following instance seems extreme because of its implied control of the writer by a publisher. A well-known writer had come from his home in west Texas for a conference in New York City. The representative of the company that had accepted his manuscript was there for their review of details. After a brief exchange of opinions on a few points, this author asked, "What are your ideas on the relationship of author and publisher? What determines your right to take from or add to a manuscript?" The response was, "We think that once we have accepted a manuscript, it is in our hands." The conference ended there. The author picked up his manuscript and it was printed soon after under the name of another publisher.

Other differences may appear. An author may suffer as a result of strong suggestions made to him for additions or changes that are presumed certain to increase sales. Advance copies reviewed by recognized critics can generate good copy for quotes in print which appear on the jacket, or by direct quotation orally over television or radio. The televised form is often in an interview with the author. The representative of the television chain conducts a carefully modulated interview with the author, during which the book is displayed. This mixture of review and advertising lends itself well to the sales purpose by having the image of the author and his personal mannerisms in the show.

A signal of hope for continuing payments to writers beyond initial royalties comes from Great Britain. A bill has been proposed by a league of writers to provide a use charge on public and rental libraries; the steady demand met by their loans and rentals would give a continuous income from use. Such aid to authors here or in Great Britain would help. Other measures are needed to improve the rights of authors in this country. Consolidation of educational and trade houses may have had a start from the subsidies given for texts on a national scale under Federal funds; or the move toward fewer and larger operations may have arisen from an inflation in costs of every item in production. A third reason may well be the stability of the school and college markets. In these and other ways the author has been brought under pressures faced also by publishers in protecting their rights.

Whatever may be the cause, or causes, today fewer titles are brought to print from the manuscripts of the scholar; what were in part prestige items in the lists of publishers are less favored. One indirect effect is on the function of university presses. More titles from these are not possible when depression circumstances make their subsidies less. Some have closed as a result, while all are under added pressures from authors who might have had outlets for manuscripts through trade channels.

These conditions greatly affect the humanities. Manuscripts are long compared with those out of the sciences. They have less popular appeal. The long-range value of studies in humanistic fields may very well be evident to a publisher, but he lacks resources to put reserve stock on his shelves for the slow, small demand of new libraries and new readers.

On the circumstances affecting personal sharing in other outgrowths from humanistic production are all the problems and promises in the performing arts; these are familiar to participants in each medium. They extend from individual appearance in speech to group productions within the repertories of music, dramatic performance, and dance. The staged play has long had here polite and unfinished handling through all degrees of professional and amateur production. Playmaking begins in childhood and continues throughout life. It is universally acceptable to audiences, from metropolitan to rural ones. Its place in American life therefore may serve as demonstration of growth possibilities in all the performing arts.

A staged play has a myriad of appeals to participants as well as to audiences. Given an adequate play text, old or modern, a director can draw out from a well-cast company the powerful appeal to arouse that favoring audience. Interpretation of roles comes out of the interplay of the director and actors. A director relies on background and on light, movement, sound, and the speech of his actors. Timing and intonation of spoken words count heavily in the total relationship across the footlights.

When the public turned toward film, first in the picture theatre and today also on television in American homes, the life of scattered playhouses ended in smaller cities and in towns along travel routes between them. A few of these musty houses still stand as relics. In many communities, as in colleges and universities, playmakers had training that brought to stage a moderate number of productions each year. A few of these folk plays written for home stages went on into all parts of the country. Class work and practical experience developed teachers and directors. The rise of this grassroots theatre was to be an important force toward the matured future of performing arts across the United States.

Local audiences in community and college theatres throughout twelve months have become a sustaining public. The groundwork for general progress in the performing arts was laid by these local and regional developments, and a new spirit of national importance developed in the life of the people. So all in the humanities came to reach the public mind through the maturing of individual desires to know and to express through the arts.

Summer centers for instruction and action in the arts have become generally sustained. At the undergraduate level, students may have courses in painting, writing, instrumental music, and dance. These have come into college and university calendars following courses well established for playwriting and for production. As such desire became vigorous in all parts of the country, there appeared the necessity for structures to serve many kinds of demand. This was met by local financing. As a result, multi-purpose buildings for all the performing arts are scattered across the United States.

Staged plays in times of peace and then of war had much to do with the spread of interest in the performing arts across this country. The multi-purpose structures have aided the movement toward Federal funding of all the arts and providing scholarships in the humanities that sustain their new growth. The extension into regional areas of all in the performing arts is today on the increase through the latest art to discover America—the ballet.

A wise worker in education, with international experiences to give him the right to speak with authority, was reviewing the nations—ancient and modern—to see how the humanities develop in them. Wickliffe Rose, an American, summed it up in four words: "The humanities take time." They grow in nations as in persons. Culture is the inner unity of a civilization. It is the spiritual synthesis of the aspects and elements of the common life.

Each generation must do more than maintain a cultural tradition; the new must be built into the living entity of the old. Rose placed his trust in universities to do this protective and creative act, and to do both through individuals. The individual human being, with his special hopes and fears, comes under the philosophy that man is a means only. The alternative is totalitarianism. The mission of the individual, in a machine age and under all other hindrances to individual growth, is to bring the arts to the general public. Wherever there is loss of balance in a society, to the lowering of concern for the aims of the humanist, even science itself suffers. Succumbing to the demands of a machine age can be as harmful as political collectivism or dictatorship. The right balance of forces can be lost and even the artist himself can be lost.

The life of the artist is the symbol of his generation. His name can be the one term of definition to relate his country to all others in human time. That quality of greatness is depicted in a passage from Joseph Conrad's essay on "The Condition of Art":

> The changing wisdom of successive generations discards ideas, questions facts, demolishes theories. But the artist appeals to that part of our being which is not dependent on wisdom; to that in us which is a gift and not an acquisition — and, therefore, more permanently enduring. He speaks to our capacity for delight and wonder, to the sense of mystery surrounding our lives; to our sense of pity, and beauty, and pain; to the latent feeling of fellowship with all creation — to the subtle but invincible conviction of solidarity that knits together the loneliness of innumerable hearts, to the solidarity in dreams, in joy, in sorrow, in aspirations, in illusions, in hope, in fear, which binds men to each other, which binds together all humanity— the dead to the living and the living to the unborn.*

This quality of universal meaning comes into society as a permanent possession first of all in the individual. It is there, out of experience in a liberal college, that the first outlines of the life of an artist often appear. Education, cultivation, and intellectual and aesthetic experience give singleness of purpose to the individual. Again, the wider outlook from life in a university hastens mind and spirit creatively—toward both scholarly aims and creative output. There are bound together all that mankind has given and is giving.

The university is the crown of every modern educational system. In a free society, it discharges with equal concern three great functions: First, it stimulates freedom of thought, perfects methods of inquiry, and promotes the advancement of knowledge through scholarship. Second, it prepares young men and women of talent, through acquaintance with the best thought and finest aspirations of all ages and peoples, for their roles

---

*The Portable Conrad, ed. Morton Dauwen Zabel (New York: The Viking Press, 1947), p. 170. Issued by Doubleday under copyright of Constable, Publishers, London.

in family and community life, in the more efficient and humane conduct of industry and government, and in the fostering of understanding and goodwill among the nations. Third, it trains selected young men and women for technical proficiency in both old and new professions, being ever sensitive to the changing and emerging needs of society. Within the free university are works out of the past that reflect the spirit of each generation of men in time. "There is one great society alone on earth; the noble Living and the noble Dead." These lines from Wordsworth portray the background of humanity at its highest and best. In the university are the resources to bring the individual into all of that great society.

The humanities come closest to the core of life. Sciences work on the structure of matter, the social sciences on the structure of society, the humanities with principles of order in the life of the individual. If we think of the humanities in their fullest sense, we realize that they draw on all that mankind has created or now creates as its record of human learning and experience. Their significance exists in two related facts— that man's spiritual, intellectual, and aesthetic experiences in the past are realities of the highest value to civilization, and that every individual in a free democracy creates his own scheme of values by uniting past learning with present experience. So long as belief in man as an individual persists, the humanities will be significant for human welfare.

The size and well-being of the world's population will be controlled to a large extent by physical and economic factors, by the available food and the products of industry, by the success of sanitation in preventing disease, by the efficiency of human organizations that will permit the most effective utilization of the total resources of the world. Ultimately, however, the determining factor for both quantitative and qualitative existence is the will to live. Belief in the future is essential if this world is to survive, and to create and strengthen this belief is one of the functions of the humanities.

Ephraim, Wisconsin
August, 1975

BRIEF SKETCHES OF CONTRIBUTORS*
TO
PART TWO: MEN AND IDEAS

*The following names, with accompanying sketches, are listed in the order of appearance in this text. The biographical information is related primarily to subjects within the text and to the years 1930-1950. References to the Rockefeller Foundation are given by the letters RF.

Eugene B. Power (p. 41) Pioneer in the development of copying and reading machines from microphotographs from the largest size down to the very small reductions for book record on cards for library use; maker of many refinements for business and technical needs. His University Microfilms at Ann Arbor, Michigan, continues storage production of educational and scholarly work. Internationally active in copying of historical documents at the earliest period of copying in such centers as the British Museum. Now active as a director of the Xerox Corporation.

Mortimer Graves (p. 54) Secretary and later director of the American Council of Learned Societies, from 1927 to retirement in 1951. He started the abstracting of translated papers from Russian into English, a project now serving a commercial enterprise for aid in all fields of knowledge from Russian sources. He developed the men and materials for wartime needs in many foreign languages, particularly in Chinese, Japanese, and Russian, as well as many less significant languages. This became basic to operations in several universities after the close of World War II. He also has served as chairman of the Committee for Aid to China, 1939-41, and as a member of the board of directors of the American-Russian Institute.

Charles B. Fahs (p. 55) Instructor and professor in Pomona College, in Oriental Affairs, 1939-45; chief of the Far Eastern Division of OSS, 1945; in the Division for the Humanities, RF, as an assistant director, 1946-50, and as director from 1950-62.

Edward F. D'Arms (p. 56) Head of the Department of Classics, University of Colorado, 1937-47; chief of educational and religious policies, Civil Affairs Division of the War Department, 1946-47; with the RF, Division for the Humanities, as an assistant director, 1947-50, and as an associate director, 1950-57. With the Ford Foundation as an officer for humanities and the arts from the start of that division in 1957 until retirement in 1970; at present an active consultant in such operations.

Charles W. Hendel (p. 57) Professor of moral philosophy both at McGill University, 1929-40, and at Yale University, 1940-59; since 1959 the Clarke professor of moral philosophy and metaphysics, emeritus, in the same university. Co-author of *Philosophy in American Education*, 1945, prepared by a committee of five chosen by the American Philosophical

Association to hold public forums of educators, clergy, businessmen, and public personalities in several places across the United States for continuing discussions of the place of philosophy in American life.

John King Fairbank (p. 60) Member of the faculty of the Department of History at Harvard since 1936; Higginson professor of history and director of the East Asian Research Center since 1959; co-author (with Edwin O. Reischauer) of *East Asia: The Great Tradition,* 1960, and author of many other works on Chinese history and politics.

Edwin O. Reischauer (p. 65) Student, University of Paris, 1933-35; studies abroad on Harvard-Yenching Institute fellowship in France, Japan, and China, 1933-38; United States ambassador to Japan, 1961-66; co-author (with John King Fairbank) of *East Asia: The Great Tradition,* 1960, and author of many other authoritative statements on the Far East.

George E. Taylor (p. 67) Historian on the Far East, and especially on China; Harvard-Yenching Institute fellow in China, 1930-32; with Central Political Institute in Nanking, China, 1933-36; in history at Yenching University in China, 1937-39; RF fellow, 1941-42; director, Far East and Russian Institute, University of Washington, 1946-49; professor of Asian studies at the University since 1969.

Herrlee Creel (p. 67) Research fellow of the American Council of Learned Societies, 1930-33; Harvard-Yenching Institute, 1931-35; in China from 1932-35 and 1939-40; RF research fellow in 1936 and 1945-46; member of the faculty, University of Chicago, 1936-70; author of eminent works on Chinese history and philosophy, including *The Birth of China,* 1936.

Robert E. Spiller (p. 71) Literary historian; chairman of the editorial board, *Literary History of the United States,* 1948, 4th edition, 1974; member of the faculty at Swarthmore College, 1921-45, and the University of Pennsylvania since 1945.

Thomas D. Clark (p. 74) Historian; member of the faculty at the University of Kentucky, 1931-68; author of books on the South, including *Pills, Petticoats, and Plows,* 1944; *The Southern Country Editor,* 1948; and *The Rural Editor and the New South,* 1948. He developed the notable series on southern travel routes from pioneer days.

Alfred Kazin (p. 75) Author and educator; Guggenheim fellow, 1940, 1947; RF fellow to study education movements in Great Britain, 1945; author of literary and historical works, including *On Native Grounds,* 1942; also has written countless critical articles; member of the National Institute of Arts and Letters.

Henry Nash Smith (p. 75) Educator and author; fellow at the Huntington Library, 1946-47; contributor to the *Literary History of the United States,* ed. Spiller, *et al.,* 1948; author of several books, including *Virgin Land: The American West as Symbol and Myth,* 1950.

Dumas Malone (p. 76) Historian; editor of the *Dictionary of American Biography,* 1929-31; editor-in-chief, 1931-36; author of books on Thomas Jefferson, notably *Jefferson the Virginian,* 1948; *Jefferson and the Rights of Man,* 1951; and *Jefferson and the Ordeal of Liberty,* 1962; all part of his five-volume biography, *Jefferson and His Time.* He was Thomas Jefferson Foundation professor of history at the University of Virginia, 1959-62, and has been biographer-in-residence since 1962.

Howard Mumford Jones (p. 81) Author and educator; professor of English at the University of Michigan, 1930-36; professor of English at Harvard University, 1936-60; editor, with Dougald MacMillan, of *Plays of Restoration and Eighteenth Century,* 1930; author of distinguished works on American literature and culture. His *One Great Society,* 1959, is a full view of present and future needs for the humanities in this country. *O Strange New World* won the Pulitzer Prize in 1964.

Samuel Selden (p. 83) Educator, author, director; began at the University of North Carolina with the Carolina Playmakers in 1927 and advanced in rank until made chairman of the Department of Theatre Arts, University of California at Los Angeles. Since retirement he has continued to write play texts and criticism.

Paul Green (p. 84) Playwright, writer, and educator. Author of folk plays and symphonic dramas on historical themes, including his 1927 Pulitzer Prize winner, *In Abraham's Bosom,* and representative symphonic dramas (his creative term), such as *The Lost Colony* (with almost uninterrupted run since 1937); *The Highland Call,* 1939-40; and *The Common Glory,* 1947. These are a few of a score that have played in their historical locations.

Albert M. Ottenheimer (p. 86) Actor; associated with the Seattle Repertory Playhouse under Burton and Florence James until 1949; currently an actor on television shows and on Broadway; he has had a principal role in *West Side Story,* appearing for several years on Broadway, on its national tour, and in Israel.

John Parker (p. 87) Educator and playwright; associate director and business manager of the Carolina Playmakers, 1936-39; he has been the director of the Junior Playmakers since 1938 and director of the Bureau of Community Drama since 1946; he directed *The Highland Call,* 1939-41, was general manager of *The Lost Colony,* 1948-51, and has been a professor of dramatic art at the University of North Carolina, Chapel Hill, since 1934.

Josefina Niggli (p. 90) Playwright and novelist; at the University of North Carolina, writing plays for the Carolina Playmakers, 1935; author of *Mexican Folk Plays,* 1938; *A Mexican Village,* 1945; and *Step Down, Elder Brother,* 1947. Her folk dramas on Mexican life are intimate and creative works of art.

Barclay Leathem (p. 93) Educator and national figure in theatrical management; executive secretary of the National Theatre Conference and civilian consultant to the Army-Navy Commission on Welfare and Recreation, 1941-45; in charge of dramatic arts at Case-Western Reserve University until his retirement.

Alois M. Nagler (p. 95) Theatre historian; came to the United States in 1938; supervised a cross-cultural survey, Intelligence Office, United States Navy, 1941-45; professor of dramatic history at Yale University since 1946 and active nationally in societies for theatrical research.

Christian Moe (p. 96) Playwright and educator; appeared in the outdoor symphonic drama *The Common Glory,* 1949-50 and 1957; since 1959 he has been professor and director of theatre at Southern Illinois University, where he maintains a diversified program of production. Recently he wrote and produced an elaborate historical play as part of the bicentennial celebration.

George C. Izenour (p. 97) Educator and inventor of lighting systems for theatre and television; lighting director, Federal theatres in California., 1938-39; RF fellow, 1939-43 and 1946-47; member of the faculty at Yale University and director of the electromechanical laboratory at the School of Drama since 1946; professor of theatre design and technology since 1960; he has designed centers for the performing arts here and abroad, and is about to have published his descriptive and illustrated survey of theatre arts buildings across the world.

John S. Diekhoff (p. 107) Educator and author; RF post-war fellow in humanities; professor of English at Queen's College from 1940-51; author of *Milton on Himself,* 1939, and *Democracy's College,* 1950.

Titles of David H. Stevens

Party Politics and English Journalism, 1702-1742. Menasha, Wis.: Banta Pub. Co., 1916. 2nd printing, New York: Russell & Russell, 1967.

The Home Guide to Good Reading. The Parents Library, Chicago: F. J. Drake & Co., 1920.

The Stevens Handbook of Punctuation. New York: The Century Co., 1923.

Types of English Drama, 1660-1780. Boston: Ginn & Co., 1923.

College Composition. New York: The Century Co., 1927.

The Teaching of College Composition. New York: The Century Co., 1927.

Milton Papers. Chicago: University of Chicago Press, 1927. 2nd printing, Folcroft, Pa.: The Folcroft Press, 1969.

A Reference Guide to Milton from 1800 to the Present Time. Chicago: University of Chicago Press, 1930. 2nd printing, New York: Russell & Russell, 1967.

The Changing Humanities: an Appraisal of Old Values and New Uses. New York: Harper & Brothers, 1953. 2nd printing, New York: Books for Libraries, 1970. Brought out in a Korean translation by the United States Information Authority, for free distribution of five thousand copies to Korean institutions.

Compiler: with Ruth Stevens, *American Patriotic Prose and Verse.* Chicago: McClurg & Co., 1917.

Compiler and editor: *A Manual of Style with Specimens of Type, containing Typographical Rules governing the Publications of the University of Chicago Press,* 8th edition. Chicago: University of Chicago Press, 1925.

Article: "Letter from Wisconsin: McCarthy on the Home Front." *The Pacific Spectator: a Journal of Interpretation,* 4 (1950), 278-87.

Index

A

Abbott, John: film story of, 94-95
Adams, John Quincy: Life of Shakespeare, 70
African linguistics: Ida Ward in, 68; missionary project in, 68
Agora: excavation of, 28; American School of Classical Studies, 112
American Council of Learned Societies: aid to, 29, 31; directors, 31, 41; operations of, 31
American Library Association: in Mexico City, 35-36; Chicago depository, 43
American School of Classical Studies, 28, 112
American studies: in first program, 29-30, 74; work in, 128 ff.
Ancient Times, 23
Anderson, Maxwell, 82
Anthropology: in Asia Minor, 111; at Lawrence University, 111; Margaret Mead's influence, 111
Arabic dictionary, 50
Archeology, 111
Armstrong, Edward G., 25
Arnall, Ellis G.: and circuit rider, 122-123
Arnett, Trevor: early years, 22; at the University of Chicago, 12; president of the GEB, 12; engages DHS, 16; his Southern program, 20; at Atlanta University, 21; methods of operation, 21-23
Arnold, Matthew: quoted, 118
Association of American Colleges, 24
Assyrian dictionary, 50
Atkinson, Brooks, 30, 82
Atlanta University, 21-22
Attolus: stoa of, 28

B

Baker, George Pierce, 129
Balance of studies: Oxford use of the term, 105; religion in the, 122
Ball, Alice D., 44
Ballet: interest in, 134
Barry, Iris, 94
Battle of the Wilderness, 5
Becker, Carl Lotus, 128
Berlin, Wisconsin: birthplace of DHS; ministry of father, 6
Berrien, William, 58
Bibliothèque nationale, 46
Bickerstaff, Knight, 66
Biographical dictionaries: American, 48-49; British, 49-50; National Endowment for Humanities and, 50
Birge, Dean: Arabic dictionary, 50
Birth of China, 66
Blanshard, Blaine, 56-57
Bloomfield, Leonard, 128
Bodleian Library: grant for, 31; Selskaar Gunn and, 102; ceremony of dedication, 102-05
Bolton, Herbert Eugene, 128
Book trade, 131-33
Books Abroad, 106
Boynton, Percy, 69
Braxton, Deacon: on Ruth Stevens, 17
Breasted, James: his **Ancient Times,** 23; his Institute, 23

143

Briggs, Le Baron, 129
British Museum: microfilm center in, 40; on catalogue of, 42-43
Brown, Gilmor, 88
Brownell, Baker, 85
Bryan, William Jennings, 57
Bush, Douglas: in Milton scholarship, 70; training, 130; on needs in
    humanities, 130
Buttrick, Wallace: Alan Gregg on, 23; in GEB, 22-23

C

Cambridge History of American Literature, 70
Canby, Henry Seidel, 70
Capps, Edward: Chicago posts, 11; support of journals, 11; Loeb ms., 12;
    consultant in humanities, 27; decennial publications, 27-28; Loeb classics, 28
Carnegie Foundation, 25
Caso, Alfonso: status in Mexico, 37; United States visits, 37; anthropological
    museum, 38
The Changing Humanities: issue in Korean, 48; quoted, 120-21
Chautauquas: in Wisconsin and New York state, 8; Harper's role in, 8;
    in Kansas, 9
Cheek, Leslie, 88
Chicago, University of: five-year grant to, 25
Civil War: effect on family, 4-5
Clark, Barrett, 88
Clark, John Scott, 10
Clark, Thomas: pioneer trails in the South, 72; comment of, 74-75; note on, 138
Colegio de Mexico: created for refugees, 36; Reyes and Villegas as sponsors,
    37; 58
Congress of chancellors, 105
Conrad, Joseph: quoted, 135
Cousins, Norman, 51-52
Craigie, Sir William A.: his dictionaries, 47
Crane, Ronald S.: literary analysis of, 71
Creel, Herrlee: at University of Chicago, 66-68; **Birth of China,** 66; comment of,
    67; note on, 138

D

D'Arms, Edward F.: war duties and in RF, 56; European influence of, 56-59;
    in the Ford Foundation, 90; comment of, 56, 111; note on, 137
Davis, Jackson: with GEB, 20, 23; in Southern Education Board, 24
Day, Edmund E.: in the GEB, 25-28; background of, 26; leaves Boards for
    Cornell University, 27
Decennial Publications: Capps and, 27-28
Delargy, James H., 107
Democracy's College, 102
Dewey, John: at the University of Chicago, 27; and Capps, 27-28
d'Harnoncourt, Renè: in Mexico, 38; in Museum of Modern Art, 33
Dickinson University, 5
Dictionaries: significance of, 46; of English, 47; of Korean, 48-49;
    Arabic, 50; 130
Dictionary of American Biography, creation of, 48; slow development of, 49
Dictionary of National Biography: Sir Leslie Stephen and, 49; new edition of, 50
Diekhoff, John S.: comment of, 101-02; note on, 140
Division Of humanities: created, 25; modes of operation, 51-55; 59-60

Dobie, J. Frank: in University of Texas, 77; in New York City, 77-78; at
    Cambridge University, 78; A **Texan in England**, 78; travels with, 79-80
Doctoral subjects in humanities, 70, 118-19
Dodds, John W., 73
Draeger, Rupert M., 40
Drama: influence of staged plays, 30; 133-34
Drew Theological Seminary, 5
Drummond, Alexander: vii, 86
Dubs, Homer, 66
Ducasse, Curt J., 50
Dulles, John Foster, 106

E

Eastman Kodak Company, 39-40
Edgerton, Franklin, 62
Elisséeff, Serge, 63
Eliot, T.S., 103
Emerson, Ralph Waldo: studies of, 70; Rusk on, 70; Phi Beta Kappa address,
    120; quoted, 120
Encyclopedia Britannica, 46
English composition: Briggs on, 129; teaching of, 131
Esdaile, Arundell, 42-43

F

Fahs, Burton: comment of, 55, 110-11; note on, 137
Fairbank, John King: in China programs, 60; comment of, 60-61; note on, 138
Far Eastern program, 60-61
Faulk, John, 108-09
Favrot, Leo M., 23
Fellowships: Donald Goodchild on, 100; postwar, 100
Film Library, 94-95
Flanagan, Hallie: in NTC and WPA programs, 30; her **Arena**, 93
Flexner, Abraham: and medical schools, 14-15; on Chicago Medical School, 14;
    on another officer, 14; in GEB and Institute, 27, 27
Flexner, Simon, 25
Foot and mouth disease, 112
Ford Foundation: support of ACLS, 31; D'Arms in, 90
Foreign languages, 112
Fort Atkinson, Wis., 5
Fort Meade, 92
Fosdick, Raymond B., 51
Founders, a play, 96
Freedley, George, 88
Fulbright, J. William, 109
Furness, Howard, 70
Fussler, Herman, 40-41

G

Gard, Robert E.: fellowship at Cornell, vii; his Wisconsin Idea Theatre and
    Regional Writers, vii; services of **passim**; comments of, 3-4; in Finland, 3;
    boyhood, 9; in three universities, 84-85
Gates, Frederick; and University of Chicago, 13; advisor to John D. Rockefeller,
    Sr., 13
General Education Board: operation of, 20-23; philosophy of, 24

Gibbon, Edward: **Decline and Fall of Rome,** 125; Echard's **History** and, 126; influence of, 126; Sir Leslie Stephen on, 126

Gildersleeve, Basil, 119

Gilman, Daniel Coit, 118-19

Gilpatric, Chadbourne, 56

Godolphin, Francis R., 102

Goodchild, 100

Goodrich, Carrington, 63

Graves, Mortimer: Russian abstracts, 53; language programs, 53-54; comments of, 54, 62-63; note on, 137

Green, Jerome, 24, 29

Gregg, Alan: on Buttrick, 23; friendship of, 25-26; director for medicine, 28; Cousins episode, 51-52

Green, Paul: symphonic drama of, 82; folk plays, 82; soldier shows, 93; White House visit, 93; comments of, 84; sketch of, 96; note on, 139

Guthrie, Tyrone, 99

H

Hale, William G., 11

Haley, Evetts: at University of Texas, 79; relations with publishers, 132

Hanford, J. Holly, 70

Haas, Mary A., 62

Hare, Richard, 66

Harper, Samuel, 66

Harper, William Rainey: at Chautauqua, 8-9; and Capps, 12; founding his university, 13; 4, comment of, 110; establishing journals, 11, 119; teaching of Hebrew, 119; and the Press, 119; quoted, from his first convocation, 123

Harvard University: five-year grant to, 25; graduate courses of 1910 in English, 10, 129; broadened basis of teaching and research in English, 70; national influence of 70-71, 129; Ivor A. Richards at, 71

Hendel, Charles W.: philosophy project, 56; comment of, 57-58; note on, 137-38

Henderson, Harold G., 63

Hendricksen, George L., 27

Hoof and mouth disease, 38

Howard Joseph Kinsey, 85

Hulbert, James Root: quoted, 11

Humanist as scholar: first materials for, 113

Humanities: definition of, 4, 117; Sarton on, 117; Rose on, 134; "will to live" and, 136

Hummel, Arthur, 66

Hutchins, Robert M.: personality, 16; policies, 16; and Stevens, 16; at Yale, 19; reception at Chicago, 19; and John D. Jr., 19

I

Ibo, 68

Indiana, University of: president of, 69; center of language study, 69

International Education Board: and Rose, 15; Palomar telescope, 23

Izenour, George: in WPA theatre, 95; extent of work, 95-97; at Yale, 95; forthcoming history of theatre structures for performing arts, 97; comment of, 97-98; note on, 140

J

James, Burton, 86

Japan: educational mission to, 99-100

146

Japanese education: Charles Johnson's comment on report, 100; Army commission, 100; request of Emperor, 100

Johns Hopkins University: five-year grant to, 25; founding of, 118; graduate studies in, 119

Johnson, Charles, 100

Johnson, Thomas H., 71

Jones, Howard Mumford: his **One Great Society**, 118; quotes Wordsworth, 118; influence of, 118; comment of, 81; note on, 139

Jones, Margo: in NTC, 30; description of, 89; work in Dallas, 89

Journals: distribution abroad, 44; Harper's innovation, 11, 119; Foundation support of, 106

Judd, Charles, 92

Judson, Harry Pratt, 27

K

Kazin, Alfred: wartime study, 75; comment of, 75; note on, 138

Kennedy, George: in Shanghai, 63; at Yale, 63; Federal restraint of, 64

King George of Greece: request of, 112

Kittredge, George Lyman, 129

Koch, Frederic: training and experience, 82; his Carolina Playmakers, 82

Korea: language, 47; dictionary of Korean, 47-48; Federal gift of **The Changing Humanities** in Korean, 48

L

Lancaster, Henry C., 25

Large grants, 31

Latin: for foreign periods of study, 113; in medieval period, 124; in 17th-century literature, 125

Lattimore, Owen: 63-64, 107

Lawrence University: life in, 9; anthropology in, 111

Leatham, Barclay: in Cleveland and in NTC, 82; in **Ten Talents**, 82; at Fort Meade, 92; at the White House, 93; comment of, 93; note on, 140

Leland, Waldo, 41

Leonard, Irving A., 58

Levi, Edward H.: on religion in universities, 122

Library of Congress: Herbert Putnam, 39; reproduction of catalog, 44; Roosevelt and Russian library, 44; Hummel and Chinese section, 66; Miss Ball's work, 44; microfilming in, 39; international influence of, 120

Linguistics: in Mexico, 38-39; in Great Britain, 68; Linguistic Atlas, 71; in this country, 128-9

Linn, James Weber, 10

Literary History, 72

Lincoln Center: financing of, 91

Lloyd James, 68

Loeb classics, 28

London School of African Studies, 68

Lowes, John Livingston: at Harvard University, 71; **Road to Xanadu**, 129-30; Neilson on, 130

Lowry, McNeil: 90

Lydenberg, Harry: work in Mexico, 35-36; as advisor, 39

M

Mabie, Edward C., 30, 80, 86

McCarthy, Joseph L., 64, 141

McKeon, Richard, 71

Stevens, David H.: enters GEB, vii; family background, 6-8; terms in office, 25; early programs of, 27; Japan report, 100; definition of humanities, 120-21; titles of works, 141

Stevens, Frank, 5

Stevens, Katherine McCoy: in Pennsylvania, 5-6; in Wisconsin, 6-8

Stevens, Ruth D.: at the University of Chicago, 17; on move to Montclair, 17; on Rockefeller Center, 17; at the Bodleian extension, 102-05; dedication to, 115

Stevens, Warren Hurst: as artist, 7, 9; as companion, 7; at college, 9; care of family, 9

Stevens, William Waters: youth, 5; Dickinson University and Drew Seminary, 5; characterized, 6; Wisconsin churches, 5-8; camps, 8

Stokes, Anson Phelps, 24, 29

Sturtevant, Edgar, 62

Swift, Harold, 13

Symphony orchestras, 112

Swadesh, Morris, 39

T

Taylor, George, 63; comment of, 67; note on, 138

Ten Talents, 82

Thesis subjects: time limits on choice, 70; change at Harvard, 129; beyond philology, 129

Thorp, Willard, 76

Tillich, Paul, 91

Turner, Frederick Jackson, 128

Turyn, Alexander, 91

U

Universities Grants Commission, 105

University of Chicago: spirit in, 4, 11

University of Chicago Press: founded, 11; Capps as editor, 12; budget of, 12

University of Colorado, 61-62

University presses: aid to, 25; leading ones, 25, 45; present difficulties of, 45

V

Vanderbilt University, 72

Veale, Douglas, 104

Villegas, Cosio: in Colègio Mexico, 36; as historian, 37

Vincent, George: at Chicago, 8; at Chautauqua, 8, 19; at Chicago dinner, 19; brief sketch of, 17-18; father of, 195; president of RF, 12

W

Waddell, Helen: life of, 23-24; honorary degree, 124; influence of, 124; quoted, 124-25

Walne, Florence, 6

Ward, Ida, 68

Weaver, Warren: wide range of influence, 28; appointment to Boards, 28; and **Scientific American,** 106

Wecter, Dixon, 73

Wells, Herman B., 69

West Side Story, 86

Whitman, Walt, 70

Wiesbaden, 107

Wisconsin Idea Theatre, vii

Y